INTO THE
HAUNTED
GROUND

Also by Anam Thubten

Choosing Compassion:
How to Be of Benefit in a World That Needs Our Love

Embracing Each Moment:
A Guide to the Awakened Life

The Magic of Awareness

No Self, No Problem:
Awakening to Our True Nature

INTO THE
HAUNTED
GROUND

A GUIDE TO CUTTING
THE ROOT OF SUFFERING

From the Tibetan Practice of Chöd

Anam Thubten

SHAMBHALA

Shambhala Publications, Inc.
2129 13th Street
Boulder, Colorado 80302
www.shambhala.com

© 2022 by Anam Thubten

Cover photo: Karen Foley Photography/Alamy Stock Photo
Cover design: Gopa & Ted2, Inc.
Interior design: Katrina Noble

9 8 7 6 5 4 3 2 1

First Edition
Printed in the United States of America

♾ This edition is printed on acid-free paper that meets the American
National Standards Institute Z39.48 Standard.
♻ Shambhala Publications makes every effort to print on recycled paper.
For more information please visit www.shambhala.com.
Shambhala Publications is distributed worldwide by Penguin Random
House, Inc., and its subsidiaries.

Library of Congress Cataloging-in-Publication Data
Names: Thubten, Anam, author.
Title: Into the haunted ground: a guide to cutting the root of suffering:
from the Tibetan practice of Chöd / Anam Thubten.
Description: Boulder: Shambhala, 2022.
Identifiers: LCCN 2021031497 | ISBN 9781611809817 (trade paperback)
Subjects: LCSH: Tantrism. | Tantric Buddhism.
Classification: LCC BL1283.84 .T48 2022 | DDC 294.3/43—dc23
LC record available at https://lccn.loc.gov/2021031497

CONTENTS

EDITOR'S NOTE

The first time I heard Anam Thubten teach, I gazed around the audience with a sense that everyone felt as personally touched as I did, as though he were speaking to each of us directly. Along with this impression was a deep appreciation for his teaching style. He has the rare gift of teaching all levels of Buddhism simultaneously. No matter how transcendent or practical the subject, his teaching continually points to the inborn nature of awakened mind and opens the gate of understanding in each of his students, whether they have been meditators for only a week or for forty years.

The aspiration for this book is to bring the seemingly esoteric and sometimes misunderstood tantric Buddhist methods of Chöd into a meaningful and personal place in the lives of its readers. Anam Thubten poignantly expresses the ineffable wisdom of this centuries-old tradition. The issues, principles, and advice laid out in this book come from within him, from the teachings he has studied, and from traditions that have ripened in his being. Over several years of attending retreats and doing volunteer work for him, it became clear to me that his teachings and his life are in harmony. He lives what he teaches; he walks the talk. His example helps us understand that regardless of our identities or our positions in society, we are all on this journey together.

This book is not only relevant for Chöd practitioners from any lineage but also eloquently presents a practical approach to everyday-life struggles. It provides direct, on-the-spot methods for working with our minds. Anam Thubten weaves anecdotes from his life into what he teaches, allowing readers to learn about their own experiences as well. We are able to develop a sincere, heartfelt understanding of this path through his descriptions of the deeper meaning of this practice. Just as Anam Thubten has woven the lineage teachings and his understanding of Chöd into his own life, through this book readers are invited to do the same.

Chöd teachings are especially relevant to the chaos and uncertainty in our world. This precious commentary is a natural outcome of Anam Thubten's Chöd teachings as they coincided with the COVID-19 pandemic of 2020. Within a week of his last teaching trip—a residential Chöd retreat in Crestone, Colorado—shelter-in-place measures were declared in California. His typical, busy travel schedule came to a halt, and he found the gift of time to write this book. It is offered as a light that may help illuminate the darkness of the pandemic, with its complexity and confusion. Between March and July of 2020, Anam Thubten dictated this entire book in a series of meetings over video calls. During these calls, he would lean back, think for a moment, and then begin spontaneously speaking the manuscript. The material flowed from and through him as a testament to his deep and precise understanding of Chöd and his love for the wisdom of Machig Labdrön, the twelfth-century Tibetan founder of the practice of Chöd. The entire content was composed in only five months. As he dictated, I had a deep sense of being in a five-month-long practice session.

Part 1 orients the reader to the background, principles, and view of Chöd that can be applied to our personal journeys, whether we are Chöd practitioners or not. In the Introduction, "Chöd in My Life," Anam Thubten shares his own journey with Chöd practice in Tibet and his experience teaching it to Westerners on retreats. Chapter 1, "Padampa Sangye's Instructions to Machig Labdrön," presents Machig Labdrön's seven pith instructions, or slogans, bringing new depth to their subtle meaning. Chapter 2, "Journey into the Haunted Ground," goes into further detail on the sixth of these instructions, specifically addressing how these teachings can bring about a deep experience of transformation in the face of the challenges of modern life. Chapter 3, "Emptiness," addresses the practice's philosophical basis of profound wisdom, without which Chöd is in danger of becoming just another pop-spirituality trend. Chapter 4, "Rituals and Liturgy" discusses the purpose and meaning of ritual in Buddhist practice and differentiates it from forms of shamanism. Chapter 5, "Vajra Dance" explains the rich method of physical movement in Buddhist practice as an expression of inner freedom and awareness. Chapter 6, "Cutting Through in Everyday Life," discusses the topic of self-reflection as a method for bringing wisdom into our daily lives. For formal Chöd practitioners and anyone who does spiritual retreats away from society, this chapter shows how to extend the experiences gained in retreat practice into the ordinary experiences of regular life. Part 2 moves chapter by chapter through the sections of *The Dakini's Laughter* Chöd sadhana by Jigme Lingpa: refuge, bodhicitta, mandala, guru yoga, feast practice, and dedication. Even though the sections are part of a particular liturgy of a formal practice, his teachings are not exclusive to it but rather present the sadhana's profound principles as life lessons. The book closes with an appendix, "Machig's Radical Path," which presents the main events of the life of the twelfth-century Tibetan founder of Chöd, Machig Labdrön.

The details of editing, illustrating, reviewing, and shaping the manuscript would not have happened without significant contributions from a few of his other students. Early on, we invited a group of Chöd practitioners to form a cohort of "first readers." They generously combed through the manuscript, chapter by chapter, asking good questions and giving practical feedback. These readers were Kay Peterson, Corey Wright, Susan Chow, Lea Barrow, and David Christie. Our gratitude to them is profound. Under Anam Thubten's kind and astute guidance, we, his Sangha, continue to carve the profound meaning of this practice into our hearts through the melodies, cadence, liturgy, and most importantly, through his teachings and guidance. The language in this book makes these authentic methods available for many to understand. From finishing stages to completion, we had the fortune of working with Anna Wolcott Johnson at Shambhala Publications. We are so grateful for her excellent ability to join her craft, her deep knowledge of the principles of Buddhism, and her gracious skill in supporting this project.

I am forever grateful to the compassionate wisdom of Ani Pema Chödrön, who insightfully suggested I listen to Anam Thubten's teachings. She sometimes references them in her own lectures, and when asked about him, she answered with love and wisdom, saying, "I think you'll resonate with him." In retrospect, this was a great understatement. He is indeed easy to resonate with! I hold deep gratitude as well to Elizabeth Namgyal, whose teachings on Prajnaparamita illuminated the profound basis of Chöd. I will always remember the wild mares of Canyon de Chelly gathering around our rugged retreat group as we sat under the umbrella of a cottonwood tree listening to Elizabeth's teachings on emptiness. The mares seemed as drawn by her deep connection and openness as we were. Her presence and their listening to these teachings spoke deeply of our interdependence with all beings, which enlivened our understanding of Chöd. It is a deep blessing that Anam Thubten and Elizabeth Namgyal lead groups into the wilderness to get to the heart of Chöd. Anam Thubten's continued commitment to his students and unfolding insights in this practice continue to inspire. I am forever grateful to these teachers and to the lineages of teachers throughout the centuries who have personally and compassionately transmitted wisdom to their devout students. May this be of benefit.

SARAH WOODARD
Albany, California, 2021

PREFACE

Homo sapiens are in some sense the funniest creatures on the planet. We have incredibly sophisticated minds that can think and analyze, but we also have the tendency to create thousands of problems for ourselves, trapping ourselves in sets of mental snarls. This is why we can be sitting on a golden decorated throne eating exquisite mangos and still be utterly miserable. This is both sad and funny. The same problem-making, sophisticated mind also comes up with all kinds of methods for solving the problems it creates. However, many of the problem-solving methods, whether religious or scientific, lack the wisdom and ability to discern the very heart of our human woes. Every now and then, though, this human mind comes up with ingenious ways to solve internal prob lems. Such skillful methods are often developed by highly evolved beings, such as yogis, mystics, and meditators.

Buddhism is rich with a variety of profound methods of working with our minds. Among them, Chöd is undoubtedly one of the most radical and powerful. Though its roots lie in ancient tantric Buddhist teachings and the Prajnaparamita sutras, it was mainly developed in the twelfth century by the well-known Tibetan scholar and yogini Machig Labdrön. Understanding her helps us understand Chöd practice. She transcended worldly concerns, such as success and fame. She was not someone merely looking for a comfortable religious compulsion or who wanted to simply sound like she had good conviction. Rather, she was fearlessly determined to precisely understand and tackle the nature of the cycle of suffering so that it could be uprooted. She did this by going inward, understanding how suffering comes into being in the first place, how our mental habits perpetuate it, and which radical methods would uproot it. She not only gained profound insight but applied her teachings and practice in real life, becoming a living example of the Dharma of love and wisdom.

The popularity of Chöd has waxed and waned throughout history. Regarded by some as an esoteric practice, at times it has been relegated to the background of people's minds. But at other critical historical moments, this powerful practice is taken up again, as an antidote to dark cultural and spiritual times. It then emerges from the recesses, directly addressing the clinging and confusion of the world. This is such a time. A Chöd revival is happening right now all over the world, in Tibet as well as other countries.

Chöd implements radical means to cut through the very core of our suffering, which is often composed of karmic and psychological entanglements. Its dynamic methods shed light on our coarse and subtle neuroses and help us to release our attachment to them physically and energetically. It is not just a bunch of fancy psycho-spiritual theories. It is creative, juicy, and powerful, as well as fun and engaging. What can be more amazing than that? One of my Western friends describes it as a playful way of letting go of ego. It has been extremely helpful for me in my personal spiritual development.

Chöd practice is a friendly approach to working with our human neuroses. This kind of approach is needed for both religious and secular people in the modern world. So many people are stuck in their internal conflict, not knowing how to bring about swift inner transformation. In Chöd, fear, jealousy, and hatred are all invited in with a spirit of love and acceptance. Not only are they welcomed in, but we even visualize offering them a feast. We imagine our neuroses in an archetypal form, like demonic beings, hungry ghosts, or green-eyed monsters. But they are not treated as an enemy within that should be suppressed. Instead, Chöd practice brings all of them into awareness with such a positive attitude that their energetic grip on our psyche is diminished.

Some religious teachings have a negative attitude toward our imperfections, encouraging us to suppress or eradicate them with an antagonistic attitude. Such an approach can have its downside. Western psychology has provided some methods to overcome mental struggles. If not for it, there would be much more craziness in this world. Being secular, psychology allows us to deal with our suffering through our own power instead of relying on a higher power. Therefore, it works pretty much for everyone regardless of their background. Undoubtedly, psychology has its own merit. Yet sometimes it is lacking in its ability to bring about radical and immediate inner liberation.

Chöd is different from any other method, and it is approachable by anybody willing to go through ground-shaking inner transformation. It has the power to take us to the very root of our problems immediately and to help us find inner liberation right there. This might sound too good to be true. One thing we must be aware of is that formal Chöd practice only works if we have the genuine willingness to go through the process it lays out. Otherwise, even if we do all its beautiful ceremonies, it will not work.

It seems that there are not too many contemporary books on Chöd. The translations of classical books can be hard for modern readers unless they are studied for a long period of time. Even for readers of Tibetan, the books can still be challenging since they might be shrouded in archaic language or complex philosophy. I have been inspired for a while to write a book on Chöd with practical and clear language. Yet teaching and travel commitments left too little time for concentrating on such a project. Then COVID-19 hit the United States, and I could not travel for many months. Like everyone else, I suddenly had all the time in the world to write a book.

In recent years, throughout the East and West, we can see monastics and lay people alike practicing Chöd in large gatherings, joyfully playing drums and bells. I feel it is important for people to understand the underlying view, or philosophy, of Chöd, to connect with the essence of these teachings, and not just do the practice mechanically. So just before beginning to write this book, I wrote and published a book on Chöd in Tibetan. I was also concerned that people in the West who were interested in Chöd would become spellbound by its ritual and methods and would misunderstand its profound meaning.

Writing this book has been a form of Dharma practice for me. I have been fascinated by Chöd from an early age, and my heart has been captured by these essential teachings all my life, especially over the last ten years. I also developed a strong affinity for a Chöd liturgy by a renowned modern master, Dudjom Lingpa, an important figure in my personal spiritual lineage. I dedicated myself to Chöd as my own spiritual practice and have been teaching it to others for many years now. I have witnessed it changing the lives of others from within. Because of my love for this Chöd path, I have spent many hours visiting ancient texts on Chöd to understand the philosophy. In doing the practice, it became closer to my heart. I believe that Chöd has the potential to utterly change our consciousness in a powerful and radical fashion, which inspired me to write this book.

It is very joyous for me—a delightful feat—to write this book and share this ancient Tibetan wisdom with others. I am happy to dedicate this book as a blessing or force that will bring about more love and more peace in this world. I dedicate it so that it will bring about a blessing that will help people find inner liberation and help this world move more quickly toward the light.

With the help of my dear friend Sarah Woodard, I was finally able to make my aspiration come true. She and I spent much time—hours and hours a day—working on this book. She shared her wisdom and tireless dedication to make sure this book was done with great care and would be as beneficial to others as possible. Sometimes we joked that we were on a Chöd marathon. There are not enough words to express the gratitude I owe her. I am deeply thankful to her for all the help she gave me with insight and devotion. May this book help others find a path to the highest freedom.

ANAM THUBTEN
Berkeley, California, 2020

PART ONE

EVERYDAY CHÖD

Introduction

CHÖD IN MY LIFE

The haunting melodies, visualizations, and methods of the ancient Buddhist practice of Chöd have been with me since childhood. Life in my hometown in Tibet during the 1980s was simple. The only audio-playing devices in my village were a few tape recorders, and very few tapes existed in the whole town. Neighbors gathered to listen to these tapes as a source of entertainment. One recording we all listened to was *The Dakini's Laughter*, a Chöd liturgy composed by the eighteenth-century master Jigme Lingpa and recorded by a contemporary lama with a wonderful singing voice. Everyone listened to it, both as a sacred chant and as our local pop folk music. I was moved by the melody even though I did not understand the meaning of the words. Now, whenever I hear the rich tunes and rhythms of this liturgy, part of it blends with my early memories. I am still deeply moved by it as an evocative, nostalgic, and beautiful experience. The sound of this liturgy takes me back to times when we lived very simply, eating barley flour and visiting with other lamas. Life was much more modest then, not as comfortable as it is now. But I was young and had lots of optimism. To me, life was like a beautiful path, strewn with flowers full of possibilities and goodness.

Many people in my hometown lived in a kind of magical world, a supernatural world full of malevolent and benevolent spirits. This was both intriguing and frightening. To us, the demons and ghosts referenced in Chöd practices were very much alive, as real as any concrete, physical phenomena. A psychic from my home region once proclaimed that he saw a horrific demon roaming around, which caused great fear in many people, including myself. I remember being quite scared at night, fearing that this demon was coming after me. Around the same time, a family in a neighboring village invited me to do a ceremony for their departed father. While there, I met a master named Lama Yeshe Wangpo, nicknamed Lama Yakwang, who was adept in the Nyingma teachings on the natural state of pure mind, also known as Ati Yoga. I asked him to give me a protection mantra to dispel the disquieting malevolent demon of the psychic's prediction. Surprisingly, he gave me no mantra. Rather, he told me that these demons were mere mental projections and that I should hold this view. From then on, my fears subsided. During lunch on that same day, he offered the *lung*, or reading transmission, of *The Dakini's Laughter* to those of us who were gathered. A reading transmission is a ceremony in which a lama reads aloud a practice liturgy, or *sadhana*, as a means of giving others permission to do the practice and bestowing upon them the blessings of the practice lineage. *The Dakini's Laughter* has thus been part of my life from an early age, not just as a sacred practice but also as a cultural art. Whenever I or others sing it, I connect with my culture and with a very special time in my life.

Part of my initial training as a monk included doing what is called *ngöndro*, the foundational practices to prepare for the

Vajrayana path. The ngöndro I was introduced to is part of the Longchen Nyingtig tradition of Dzogchen practice, the innermost secret teachings of the nature of mind practiced by many monks and nuns in the Nyingma lineage. The Nyingma school is considered the ancient school of Tibetan Buddhism, and its practice texts use the earliest translations of the Buddha's teachings from Sanskrit into Tibetan. The Nyingma practice of ngöndro includes performing a total of five hundred thousand accumulations of different practices, including one hundred thousand prostrations. Unlike other sects, this ngöndro also includes a brief Chöd practice, using *The Dakini's Laughter* liturgy. Though there are many beautiful Chöd liturgies, it feels like this one landed on me without me seeking it out. It came to me early in life and has been part of me constantly, even though I would not do it as my primary practice for many years to come.

In Tibet, Chöd has been typically regarded as a Dharma of vagabonds, wandering yogis, or holy beggars. While many Tibetan monks and nuns do this short Chöd practice as part of ngöndro, a rare few do it for their whole lives, living as wandering Chöd practitioners, or Chödpas. In the old days, these Chödpas wandered everywhere, practicing in various haunted grounds away from society but at the same time serving important roles in society as well. People knew who they were, and communities supported them. Our modern world does not readily accommodate wandering yogis—as it is difficult to survive without a passport or ID, walking around begging for food—but in some places today you can still encounter them, living freely, tuned into big mind that can handle anything. Nothing shocks or terrifies them. These days, it seems the image of Chöd is changing in Tibet. Though the Chödpa's journey is typically done alone, there are masters who are supremely adept at these practices and who gather students into a loose community. When these groups are formed, they are subject to the same politics and power struggles seen in other communities. We can find large assemblies of well-shaven monks and nuns in revered monastic communities who are well trained practitioners playing the instruments like a Buddhist orchestra. This was not as prevalent in the past.

At an early age in Tibet, I met a Chödpa whom my family had invited to do a ceremony for the dead. He lived near a cemetery, and his job was to chop up dead bodies. My family also invited a group of monks, dignified in their robes and displaying great comportment. The Chödpa was much more earthy. He never washed his hands. He ate and drank out of a cup made from a human skull, while the monks were served in beautiful cups. I was relieved and appreciative when I was served in one of the beautiful cups, too. The Chödpa intrigued me, but though I secretly admired his freedom and his utter lack of conventional social constraints, I did not want to become like him. I never would have suspected then that Chöd would become so central to my life.

When I moved to the United States and began to create a home base in California, I started teaching slowly, organically. In the beginning, I held small group gatherings, primarily teaching meditation and sadhana. I did not have any plan to teach Chöd, but my early connection to it haunted me, and it gradually came more strongly into my mind. Eventually, I would follow this inner guidance and bring groups of Western practitioners to wild places like Canyon de Chelly to do Chöd practice together.

―――

Earlier in life, even while doing ngöndro, I had developed little understanding or affinity with Chöd. Sometime after 2000, it came back into my mind, with a strong longing to reconnect. This inspired me and a few others to depart for a Chöd retreat. I felt that it would be powerful to do a Chöd retreat in the same way it was done in the past, which is to go on a pilgrimage and camp out in different spots in the wilderness. A group of seven of us decided to do this together in the Southwestern United States, because that part of the country is beautiful and at the same time stark and wild. We drove to Jemez Springs and Angels Peak in New Mexico and Canyon de Chelly in Arizona.

The pilgrimage started because I was feeling that something different was needed in my spiritual practice. I felt a strong intuition that my consciousness had to be shaken from the root to be transformed and crack open. I felt that I had been doing my spiritual practice mechanically, as a compulsion. There was a deep need for my practice to be more alive in my life. I felt that by doing something radical, I could break the barricade. I was curious to leave the familiar milieu behind and go to a totally wild and new environment to see what would happen.

I do not know why the others decided to go along with me. I was not teaching so much at the time. Even though we were traveling together, there was a shared sense that we were traveling deep into solitary and wild places to delve into an inward spiritual journey on our own. We gathered a few times a day for teachings and a meal, but the seven of us tried to camp as far away from each other as we could to make sure we would not have too much reassurance and comfort from our companionship. Traditionally, intensive Chöd retreats are done in places that are referred to as "haunted grounds," or *nyensa*. These are places that can challenge us, often rugged country with rough terrain usually in the wilderness.

Navajo Nation has a rich history of the civilization of their ancestors who lived there. Traveling there, we became their guests. Given the sovereignty of the Navajo Nation, we were foreigners, traveling in a foreign land. It was meaningful to witness the dominion of this Native nation embedded within the United

States. Even though most of the retreat participants were Americans, none of us were Native Americans, and so it was necessary to have Native guides. Our guide on the first trip to Canyon de Chelly was a medicine woman, with a noble and powerful presence and a strong and dignified spirit. We felt she was there to protect us and that nothing bad could happen under her shelter. Each morning as I taught, she listened deeply.

After the trip into the canyon, our guide invited me and my friend to visit her home on the reservation. She shared with me her thoughts on the spiritual connectedness between our two traditions—Tibetan and Navajo. I was shocked by how simple and basic her home was, without much furniture. Until then, I had not seen people living like this in the United States, one of the richest countries in the world. It was eye-opening for me to see the poverty of the Navajo community. After our wonderful time on retreat, seeing this brought me sadness that their culture is deteriorating, not thriving. Much later, I learned that this woman had passed away, and I was filled with gratitude that she had guided us into her sacred land and blended in with our group with such respect.

When I returned to the same place in later years with larger groups, our guides were always accommodating and helpful. Their gentleness and strength gave us a sense that we were welcomed in their land and that we were under their protection. They often camped near us, just on the periphery of our widely dispersed encampments. They knew exactly where to position themselves to protect us from wild bears and mountain lions, who roamed around after nightfall. At first, we were alarmed by the crack of gunshots in the night, but we came to understand that our guides were scaring the wild animals away and protecting us. As the days flowed together, they became like our sacred protectors, or *dharmapalas*, guarding our practice. They became part of our group, and we felt a strong bond grow between us. When we departed, we grieved leaving them behind. They had shared their history and personal lives with us. They also shared their Navajo spiritual beliefs, stories, and myths, which helped us understand more about the history of the canyon and the centuries-old human connection with that land. Personally, I feel sadness now and then from witnessing the traumas they lived through, the invasion of their land, and the near destruction of their culture. Because of this, they are one of the most disenfranchised groups in modern times, like many indigenous cultures around the world.

During the opening of a later Chöd retreat, a singer and elder in the Navajo tradition named Leon Skyhorse Thomas joined us and offered a sacred ceremony to bless our retreat. He asked me to stand nearby so that he could bless me and my ritual Tibetan drum, bell, and trumpet. I clearly remember him chanting the well-known Navajo "Beauty Way" prayer. He asked us to repeat after him the phrase "Walk in beauty." There was a moment where we felt an energetic harmony flowing among us from witnessing these two traditions blending in our circle. This was reassuring, considering that the history of their land was of being occupied by foreigners and struggling with their sovereignty. We did not want to do anything disrespectful to them. I felt that he gave us permission, on the spot, to enter their sacred land and do Chöd practice.

The landscape of Canyon de Chelly was breathtaking to me, and I had never seen anything like it in my life. Physically it is gorgeous, with tall formations of sandstone standing on each side, in stark contrast to my usual environment. I was constantly mesmerized by the sandstone formations, the colors, and the intriguing shapes. We all felt like we had landed on a different planet. Simultaneously, my spirit was uplifted, and a sense of joy arose by seeing the wonderous scale and magnitude of the canyon cliffs, which blew my mind. At the same time, there was deep discomfort, and we felt we were in unfriendly territory.

In my life, I have done many ceremonies and sadhanas with an assembly of monks in a temple. I love the rituals, art, sacred images, and the beauty and blessings of temples. In Canyon de Chelly, however, practicing outside in the wilderness with few companions and no temple walls was like discovering a vast interior temple, filled with natural sacredness. This was the beginning of my true relationship with Chöd, though it was still in an embryonic stage. While I knew the philosophy intellectually, I did not have a clear idea of why I was starting it or what was inspiring about it. I felt that Chöd was the right path for me, but it would not be an easy one. In that sense, choosing this practice when it was so challenging may seem contradictory. Part of me had resistance, but I knew that I could not change my mind at that point, because it was too late. I had already recognized my connection to it and wanted to understand its meaning viscerally, from deep in my heart.

On our first trip, there was both a feeling of tremendous joy and of continual discomfort. Practicing in the wilderness—without familiar sanctuary, order, and style, with no altar, no elaborately decorated roof, no sacred statues, and no temple seating—made the experience very uncomfortable. It was disquieting. I was challenged by how wild it felt sitting under a tree on the dirty, dry ground, exposed to the elements. As we settled into being there, our minds also began to settle. The canyon's magic became our sacred temple. We found it deeply liberating to do this powerful practice in the open air, with the sky as our ceiling, the earth as our floor, and the magical sand formations like ancient *stupas*. The tree that we practiced under was the pillar of our temple. As we played our musical instruments, we heard them echo through the canyon, stirring our yearning for awakening.

My friend Elizabeth Namgyal brilliantly co-taught these retreats with me, contributing her profound understanding of emptiness and her courage to dismantle illusions. Everyone, both teachers and students, sat on the same level of ground, with no hierarchy. I felt I did not have to impress anybody, and nobody seemed to be trying to impress me either. It was joyful to experience the world free from politics and the hustle and bustle of the city. There was a feeling that I was alone, cut off from human civilization, completely isolated. In that sense of being alone, it was much easier to get to know myself, explore who I am, and see all my karmic and psychological patterns.

Nonetheless, I sorely felt the absence of my familiar environment. There was a continual haunting sensation just below consciousness that something was missing. It could have been as simple as missing a warm bathtub or a delicious hot dish of ravioli. This sense of something missing was also part of the discomfort, part of the sense of shaking my consciousness to allow it to open to a new level. I remember the happiness I felt from being in the pure natural world, away from human drama. But at the same time, I realized how attached I was to people, good food, a comfortable bed, and reading books. These were not available. This was the first challenge that confronted me. An insight dawned in me at the way we human beings can be lost in comforts, physically and psychologically.

Many people take solo spiritual retreats in beautiful, well-appointed retreat houses but do not challenge themselves out in the wild. Even doing deep practice is still a secure and comfortable experience when done in a nice cabin. Being in the wilderness, in a tent, and moving from one place to another really takes you out of your comfort zone. As part of Chöd practice, we try not to tend to our daily, personal rituals like makeup, shaving our beards, and looking into mirrors. On our first trip to the canyon some of us took showers outside, but during later trips we tried not to do this. As much as possible, we left our personal rituals behind, focusing instead on the practice itself. What I learned from this is that we are always trying to fix our images every day. We constantly try to meet a standard about how we should look. It is like a duty that we are all bound by. It comes along with lots of pride, shame, and judgement, and we lose our ability to see others for who they are and accept the way we are.

It took hours to hike into and get back out of the canyon. There was no escaping the raw encounter with our own minds and deeply embedded neurotic patterns. The scale of the canyon was quite freeing, helping us shed our busy minds, little by little. It invited us to experience spaciousness; time stopped and allowed us to go deep within ourselves, because nothing from outside could interrupt the inner journey. The environment allowed us to see whatever was in our psyches, both light and darkness. There were no mindless pleasures to get lost in. There were none of the routine daily chores to escape in. In an unfriendly environment, and with the right intention to explore who we are, we are inspired to meet our inner darkness, to meet everything we usually try to escape from. We are invited to go through a big transformation and see a whole new dimension of who we are, beyond ego, persona, and identities: the place in which we are simply pure consciousness, inseparable from everything else.

Most people in our group were relatively healthy, but one, a very good friend of mine, was dealing with terminal cancer. I had lived with him and his family for quite a while. They kindly fed me and gave me shelter. Though he had been diagnosed with terminal cancer before the retreat, he was not accepting what the doctors told him. I felt that he was trying to prove he could overcome it with everything he did. At first, he was in denial of his situation, but it was clear that the rugged environment was difficult on his body. Through the power of the Chöd practice, I felt he began to accept the reality of his illness over the course of the retreat. He died not long after the trip, and I felt that during the retreat he had consciously made peace with his mortality. By presenting these teachings in diverse places and to different cultures of people, I found that Chöd's inherent principles transcend culture and context. The people I met at retreats were sincere and brave, willing to leave their comfort zone to embark on an inner journey. They were not just seeking entertainment or looking for an external savior to solve their problems. Their keen intelligence and subtle understanding of Buddhism allowed me to feel comfortable sharing the practice with them.

These days, I feel that Chöd is growing stronger and stronger inside me. My first and following pilgrimages to Canyon de Chelly allowed me to ripen my practice so that I can use it in everyday life. I apply its powerful and direct methods to work with my mind and to encourage understanding in others who come to my meditation retreats. Chöd has been continually in my life in some way since that first trip to Canyon de Chelly. It has waxed and waned, organically fading from and then returning to the forefront of my consciousness, as though I have an unbroken sacred contract with it.

1

Padampa Sangye's Instructions for Machig Labdrön

It is said that all Tibetan Buddhist teachings came from India except for Machig Labdrön's version of Chöd. Not only did she establish it in Tibet, but some say her distinct Chöd wisdom is the only Buddhist teaching that journeyed back to India from Tibet. She developed her Chöd teachings as a student of the Prajnaparamita sutras on emptiness, then as a scholar and accomplished yogini. She had three main masters in her life, one of whom was the Indian yogi Padampa Sangye. She received many teachings from him, but it was the advice he gave her on their first meeting that would be the true compass guiding her throughout her life. It deeply influenced her inner development and was the source of inspiration for her form of Chöd practice.

On Machig Labdrön's first meeting with Padampa Sangye, she showed customary respect by trying to bow to him. However, he in turn recognized her as an extraordinary being. Touching foreheads with her, he refused to receive her bow, indicating that he saw her as his equal. Through their profound exchange, Machig Labdrön requested teachings and Padampa gave her seven axioms as his essential advice: reveal your hidden faults, trample on what challenges you, cultivate what seems impossible, cut your fetters, let go of attachment, journey into the haunted ground, and realize mind like sky. These axioms became the basis for her lifelong spiritual practice.

1. REVEAL YOUR HIDDEN FAULTS

We all have places where we are blind to our inner motivations, psychological baggage, and the games of ego. In everyday life, the impulses behind many of the things that we do and our emotions arise from the unconscious. We often have no clue as to why we do what we do or feel what we feel. The power of the unconscious keeps us blind to true self-knowing. Though there are many things we do know about ourselves, there is still a great uncharted part of our being that is not usually exposed. This is a shocking proposal to many people because they tend to think that they know themselves. If you tell them that they do not know themselves, it could lead to an argument with unwanted consequences. As we begin to tread on the spiritual path, we inevitably come to the realization that there is a vast territory filled with unconscious impulses and karmic patterns like wild beasts roaming around in a jungle.

Sometimes we can be conscious of our motives and psychological patterns, but we do not confront them directly due to ego's resistance. We let them continuously govern our lives. For example, spiritual people may harbor hatred in their hearts and know all the reasons and deeper issues for why it is there. Even though they can trace the root back to early childhood, upbringing, or karmic stuff, they may still be complacent and not confront its source. In this way, ego is able to continuously resist authentic inner transformation. When we directly confront our issues with an attitude of acknowledging the problem and being determined to work through it, we gain a new impetus propelling us to inner freedom.

This first piece of advice is all about being honest with ourselves and directly confronting our *kleshas*, the conflicting emotions or inner poisons. These are mental states that afflict the body and mind, experienced as disruptive forces that often incite us to unwholesome actions. The five root kleshas are ignorance, attachment, aversion, pride, and jealousy. But here, it is also important to understand the Tibetan word for "fault," which is *tsang*. It means wrongs or mistakes, particularly those that we keep to ourselves and do not expose to others. In colloquial Tibetan, *tsang* often refers to some sort of shameful dirty story, like when we say someone is "hiding something." These may be stories about a family member who did something that could be seen as embarrassing in the context of a cultural value system, like mispronouncing a word in front of everyone or losing control of a bodily function at a party. Or it could be more serious than that, such as your brother stealing a yak from your uncle. This may be the kind of thing that is gossiped about by your neighbors, who entertain their kids with it or use it as ammunition against you after you have a falling out.

In Buddhist writings, *tsang* refers to your own faults—conflicting emotions that you are totally unconscious of or that you know about and are unwilling to confront. When we start on any kind of true spiritual path, what we really do is begin to bring psychological and karmic patterns to light in order to uproot and become free from them. Without this process, there are not too many doors for inner transformation. Regardless of what we do, we will not change inside. We may be outwardly spiritual and holy, doing fancy practices and religious observances, but our internal patterns can remain intact. We are like thieves who go to jail for stealing, are released, and go right back to stealing. Our imprisonment did nothing to reform us because we did not self-reflect or learn from our mistakes. Basically, we did not discover our inner impulses and motives for our misbehavior, so they continue to dictate our behavior.

The use of the word *tsang* is quite interesting, with many nuances. It does not really directly indicate that conflicting emotions are bad—just that we have a propensity to hide them. The important question is why we try to hide and avoid confronting our patterns and revealing them to ourselves. This has two reasons. We have been living so unconsciously that even the ideas of self-reflection and self-knowledge are not part of our paradigm. This is a kind of innocent lack of awareness of how profoundly we are driven by our deeply rooted patterns. Or we may have an understanding of the importance of self-knowledge and the significance of true inner transformation but still resist facing our problems, which is where ego steps in. Ego blocks the whole process of revealing. Ego is okay being spiritual as long as spirituality does not involve bringing our inner poisons to the light of awareness. This has to do with the fact that our ego and personality are formed of these conflicting emotions, so bringing them to awareness would mean dismantling itself. The path is about going beyond ego's tactics of hiding from itself. We should never underestimate its tenacity and strategy to keep its ground built of old patterns.

There are numerous anecdotes about how people thought they were spiritual and enlightened but were in fact seduced by their own ego. There is a story about the nineteenth-century master Patrul Rinpoche working on a complex visualization of a sacred configuration of tantric Buddhist deities. Because of his level of training, he was adept at visualization practice and easily developed complex images in his mind. If there were a Buddhist talent show, he would have won due to his amazing mental prowess and would have impressed the whole audience. However, he was unaware that he was fixating on this ability and became proud of himself. When he reported to his teacher, his teacher started yelling at him and kicked him out. Patrul was so shocked at this reaction that he lost the ability to visualize, along with his pride over his achievement. His teacher did him a great favor by exposing where he was stuck.

It is significant to say that we reveal our own hidden faults—not someone else's. Revealing hidden faults does not mean exposing someone else, calling them out in public, or telling your guests that your partner snores or is angry. This is an inward journey of self-honesty. It requires bravely facing all the squirrely places in your mind and thoroughly owning them.

In the teachings on radical self-knowledge, all faults should be dug up, actively revealed, and acknowledged with commitment to work on them. It means to go inward and bring the light of awareness to things we have been hiding with ulterior motives. But do not think that this is a journey filled only with hardships—it is the other way around. There is tremendous joy once we commit to this inner work—so much that we will feel that our whole being cooperates in moving toward freedom.

2. TRAMPLE ON WHAT CHALLENGES YOU

Fear and resistance are often the forces that hinder our inner growth, holding us back from experiencing a greater sense of freedom and from exploring the endless magic of existence. Moving beyond them creates the possibility of not living in the cocoon of comfort and habits. We often take refuge in a comfortable physical environment and in familiar realms of consciousness. From these places, we do not dare to enter the unknown and become locked up in a habituated internal and external world. Sometimes this habituated world can be quite comfortable, but at the same time there is an abundance of suffering in it. It continues until the roots are cut. People choose life lived in this familiar realm and get very attached to it, which then strengthens their resistance to exploring the unknown world. Here, Padampa advises Machig Labdrön to invite the unknown and to drop fears and resistance right on the spot, immediately. Chöd is about intentionally inviting and embracing the unknown, facing it, then dropping all resistance to it.

To "trample" is to tread on and crush—to destroy on the spot. It is an immediate approach without hesitation or mercy, directly confronting and conquering fear and resistance. There is a sense of testing your edge. The truth is that we have an extraordinary ability to conquer our resistance if we have the will to do so. Most of us may be able to remember that there have been life challenges we thought we could not overcome. At those times, we may have found the will to conquer them with a sense of triumph. Those moments of triumph can be an empowering reminder that, with commitment and willingness, we have the ability to overcome our challenges.

Trampling is a powerful image for bringing whatever is intimidating you under your foot—trampling on it with humor and fearlessness. To meet fear directly and radically without analysis often requires a great deal of courage. It is based on the view that the challenges are created by ego rather than having any intrinsic reality. With that view, the commitment is to not give in to ego or its delusions and confusions. You sense that you are no longer your ego, even though you have been experiencing fear, resistance, and everything that ego constructs as your reality. Then, there is space between you and your ego, and you have the ability to break the ego's shackles on your consciousness.

In general, there are two ways of working with challenges. The first is the gradual process of recognition. Typically, many people use psychological and spiritual analysis—journaling or talking to a therapist or spiritual mentor—as ways to address their fears and inner demons. No doubt, deeper self-awareness develops through this approach. But at some point, it becomes like chewing on the issues, an obsession in itself—almost like the problems are talking about themselves.

Here, Padampa is not suggesting the gradual self-help approach. From the point of view that our mind's nature is already free, Padampa is presenting a second method—radically and directly facing your challenges. You do not indulge them but go straight into them to conquer them. He is not demanding an impossible mission but is just reminding us that all we need is to be free from the self-imposed trap of ego, because many of our challenges are simply part of ego and do not exist in the realm of reality itself.

We do not have to go looking for resistance and challenge; there is plenty of it in us. So whatever challenge shows up, the moment you recognize it, trample on it on the spot. The point is that if you are resistant to letting go of fear, just let go of it. If you are afraid of love, just let go of your resistance to it. Open your heart and take in the soft and nurturing outpouring coming toward you. If you are afraid to speak in public, just take your seat and use your voice— say what is true and meaningful. Someone once asked Shunryu Suzuki Roshi, a famous Japanese Zen teacher, "What is hell?" He replied, "Hell is having to read aloud in English." What challenges you may not be a challenge to someone else. We human beings are distinct from each other, beyond our commonalities as a species.

One time a friend of mine had trouble with someone he worked with. As we all know that when a friend tells us about something like this, we tend to immediately jump on our friend's side, even if we are not asked. We may begin to judge the other person without ever having met them. Ego loves to take sides. But my friend gently said, "He is a creature of complexity." This showed he was insightful and not reacting to the difficult coworker but recognizing his issues without taking them personally. We are all creatures of complexity! We are born with karma and are neurologically, genetically wired to react in certain ways, and then we are influenced by nature and nurture. Biological, cultural, and social circumstances make us prone to different strengths and challenges. Nonetheless, it is by trampling on whatever our unique limitations are that we find the freedom to compassionately understand others with this all-encompassing wisdom of human conditions.

A whole host of fears visit us every day. Usually they show up as stress, depression, and nagging anxiety. Your friendships or relationship may be filled with pain, with serious betrayal or miscommunication, but you may be afraid to open a direct and honest discussion about it. Your fear makes reconciliation and understanding impossible. From this fearful place, friendship cannot be restored but can be lost for years. Our ego has thousands of strategies for avoiding conflict, such as ignoring, being busy, cocooning in our spiritual practice, indulging in mindless entertainment, or engaging in gossip to numb ourselves. Sometimes, ready or not, life forces us to trample on challenges, even without ceremony or ritual or help from a master. We may have to jump, regardless of our paralyzing fear. There are times for other more elaborate methods, but this simple and direct strategy often works. We also have to acknowledge who we are, that we are not superhuman beings able to transcend all limitations, and that there is vulnerability in us that has to be cherished. Sometimes we are not able to cut through right on the spot, and sometimes we are.

When I was young, I was very heady and loved to study. By contrast, many of the boys in my village were more physical and reveled in taking risks. But I was more domestic and did not play in the landscape, testing myself against nature like they did. One time I heard that while the boys were in the mountains herding their yaks, one strayed away from the herd. The village boys heroically searched for it, slept in the mountains all night, and did not return until morning. At the time, I was impressed that they could do this, because to me it was a scary scenario and I could not imagine doing it myself. Sometime later, on a nighttime journey through the dark Himalayan landscape, I met this fear again in a way that I could not avoid. I was traveling with a few people, and we had to cross a narrow bridge over a strong flowing river. It was the only way across the river, and turning back would have been a failure in my mind. Having dealt with this sort of situation before, my friends easily crossed the bridge. I was so scared, though, that I felt I could not do it. I was shaken with the fear of falling, being injured, or dying. Fear rushed through my system, my body shook, and I recited some prayers. While the prayers helped me calm down, they did not make my feet move. Finally, I heard a voice in my head say, "Just do it! There is no turning back!" So, I did. I crossed without falling down.

For many people this would not be a big deal, but for me it felt like a symbolic initiation. Something happened in me after that experience—a feeling that I could trust myself to be strong when necessary. This is not something I should brag about, because by many people's standards this challenge is not a big deal at all. Most people have had similar experiences of running into difficulties and overcoming their usual egoic blocks against being brave and wise. By encountering these and overcoming them, you begin to trust in yourself. You may not even be conscious that you are developing this trust.

What Padampa is saying is that stepping into what challenges us can help us intentionally let go of fears on the spot. You must hold an attitude of sacred confidence, or heroism, and make a radical change in your consciousness. This will give you freedom from the shackles of fear. Trampling on challenges is also about encountering and conquering our limits. For example, you may be afraid of heights without even knowing it. You might like to find out where the edge of that fear is and then do something radical to test and overcome it instead of letting it run your life. This is not encouragement to become a reckless daredevil just to prove something to yourself. Daredevil behavior is simply another trap of ego—proving dominance over danger. The egoic motivation is to prove that you are stronger or have more physical prowess than the average Joe. But with genuine motivation, the whole process becomes an inner initiation through which you develop a new level of courage. This will have a positive impact in your life.

3. CULTIVATE WHAT SEEMS IMPOSSIBLE

There are situations in our lives that feel impossible to overcome or transcend. Whether this is true or not, we shape our relationship to what seems impossible by telling ourselves a story that such a condition cannot change or that we lack the ability to transcend it. Given that, our consciousness may become limited by our fixed perceptions—we see what we think we should see and feel what we think we will feel. Though the limitations seem real in our minds, as if woven into the law of reality, changing our perceptions can transform and dissolve them.

Each of us has a sense of the impossible in our minds, made of internal and external conditions that we feel are intrinsically real. We label them as either good or bad and therefore feel we cannot go beyond them. The ones we regard as dark may appear to be so powerful that we give ourselves unconscious permission to succumb to their spell, holding a belief that they are more powerful than our ability to overcome them. Sometimes we maneuver around them to avoid confronting them, without ever authentically letting them go or truly transforming them. Things are not intrinsically how they are being perceived by us. Our previous experiences, thoughts, feelings, and beliefs prejudice how we perceive and abide in the world. These fundamentally erroneous perceptions are projected onto the outside world and onto how we see ourselves. In other words, there is no doubt that we have conventional understanding and insight about the world and ourselves, which holds some truth in its own way, yet such a state of mind creates a false paradigm of impossibility. This paradigm can be called duality, or samsara, or the boogeyman in our heads.

By radically uncoupling the object of perception from our conditioned projections, we come closer to experiencing things in their own nature. When that happens, everything about the world and ourselves, including conflicting emotions, would be seen from a completely different point of view. This would give us the experience of being able to transcend the sense of the impossible, through which we might be able to face conditions and overcome our reactions. We can drop our preferences and welcome whatever comes in the spirit of equanimity and openheartedness. Even our own conflicting emotions would be seen in a different light, in which they are neither intrinsically good or bad, but are primal forces, not separate from the universe or nature. Such seeing will allow us to directly engage with them, so that they can be transformed into a force we are not bound to anymore.

The illusion of impossibility prevents us from discovering what lies beyond mundane reality, in which we are often caught up in aversion and attraction, like and dislike, and endless preferences. We open to the possibility of a higher, more spiritual meaning of life. We become bigger inside. This expands our love and our ability to go beyond concepts and beliefs around good and bad, or possible and impossible, which are often simply the game of ego.

Padampa is again inviting us to take a radical approach here, to work with the idea of the impossible and remember that each of his pieces of advice to Machig Labdrön was radical. He is not asking us to reflect inside and find out what is being held as impossible in our minds, then work with each one step by step, taking as much time as needed. Instead, he is demanding that we deliberately face what is being held as impossible, and then right there, while closely dancing with the demon of impossibility, transcend it on the spot. He is also asking us to deliberately do something radical by inviting the very situations we previously avoided. We actively seek out moments in which our minds stop and possible/impossible references are left behind as mind soars in vast unconditioned freedom. Whatever limits you from becoming free—confront it. See how this radical approach changes the whole situation. When something scares or repulses you, turn and look into the face of the fear and aversion, feel it flood through you, and stay present to the coursing, vibrant energy, rather than turning away. You will then experience sudden liberation from fear and aversion.

Do Khyentse Yeshe Dorje was a great Dzogchen master known for being unconventional and was the guru to the renowned teacher Patrul Rinpoche. He revealed a Chöd sadhana in which some of these slogans are included. He rephrased this one as "Savoring what seems impossible." This is more than just pushing yourself to face the inner limitations that scare or repulse you. It encourages us to develop an attitude that we are going to turn these limitations into a fantastic divine feast. We develop an attitude of running toward them, savoring them with joy and ease, and transmuting everything into pure sacred experience, without even the sense that we are facing a challenge. From this, you know that you can savor all things, even those that used to be challenging. Since Chöd is radical, it invites us, as tantric alchemists, to transform dust into gold and turn waste into fertilizer. We are able to enjoy or be okay with things our ego dislikes or even has absolute aversion to. Then, everything that seems impossible becomes possible.

4. CUT YOUR FETTERS

Here Padampa encourages Machig Labdrön to first cut attachment to home, belongings, and even to her community. Cutting your fetters is not to be misunderstood as a form of detachment. Detachment means to close your heart and give up any feeling for others. Cutting through fetters is far from this. The wisdom of nonattachment does not reject human emotions and feelings such as love, closeness, and affection. The Tibetan word *triwa* refers to attachment to and dependency on our known world, specifically to our friends, family, community, and our home. It is something that you are hooked by and want to keep coming back to—mainly, people, possessions, and relatives. This axiom means to cut through how you are hooked by family and personal relationships. We often define our selves, our sense of "I," through who and how we are related to other beings. In this sense, the relationship becomes a fetter, constraining our interior lives. Ego relies on this sense of a separate "me" and can identify with anything as "me" or "mine."

Padampa's instructions are to cut fetters so that there is no longer an intrapsychic binding or identification with home, possessions, and friends. It does not mean to literally drop them but rather to cut through the egoic bondage to them. This trap can hinder us from maturing and growing. In contemporary language, such a trap blocks the path of self-actualization. To be clear, the term *self-actualization* used in modern psychology is different from enlightenment, but it helps us begin to understand this axiom. The emotional bondage must be let go of to find spiritual maturity. The bindings of attachment hold you back from expanding your heart and mind. They often generate grasping, anger, jealousy, resentment, false certainty, and codependence. The Western world may have a hard time understanding Buddhist notions of renunciation and letting go of egoic attachment to family members. When misinterpreted as detachment and rejection, it can seem heartless. But the point is not literally giving them up. Rather, "letting go of fetters" encourages us to let go of the trap of attachment itself. Then, relationships do not hinder us from growing inside.

We see this clearly in young adults who leave home for the first time and experience a radical unbinding of identity. Entering the world without their parents, siblings, and familiar childhood furnishings, they enter great uncertainty. The shift in identification can be so strong, it can leave the young adult feeling utterly unmoored from how they once identified themselves. Some may crack up during their first year away from home. "Freshman madness" is a term used to describe first-year college students who come unglued, act out, and become unstable trying to navigate the world without the familiarity of their early lives. Yet, striking out on their own also gives them the chance to open their minds and hearts to full maturity.

Dependency, the egoic attachment itself, can become a psychological cradle in which the psyche hunkers down, not daring to explore the world. Letting go of fetters challenges the familiar trap of convenience and coziness, though we rarely stop to closely examine how our comfort zone is constructed. The simplest act of sleeping alone in the wilderness, even for a few nights, could be very challenging to ego, not only because of missing luxuries but also because the house, career, and relationships that we usually identify with are no longer there. It exposes our fundamental aloneness, which is always there and has never been trapped by anything. Through letting go of fetters you discover who you are, overcoming the need for constant confirmation from outside. It requires a radical approach that may seem either courageous or heartless. Stepping away from our comfort zone can help us wake up to how attachment and fear cause us to shrink inside. Then when we return to our familiar world, we become more present to healthy interdependence between ourselves, the people we love, and the world.

Though the path of cutting our fetters may not sound enticing, it turns out to be the most liberating, because it is the doorway to absolute freedom in which we begin to know unconditional happiness. Our freedom is not dependent on anything else. We are who we are.

5. LET GO OF ATTACHMENT

Pain and pleasure are part of our biological survival at a basic level. It is not something that only humans experience; animals experience this too. Our life begins with our ability to feel pleasure and comfort: we are nurtured, eat food, and then experience all the sense pleasures that are part of life. Music, smelling flowers, tasting delicacies, wearing fine soft clothes—all these sense pleasures have to do with our biological striving to survive. We are a species that tends to be pleasure seeking and pain avoidant. Enjoying sense pleasures is normal and healthy and good for our survival. Often what is pleasurable to us also helps us live a long life. But this is not always true. Food is a good example: some intoxicating substances may be pleasurable, but pleasure can also be poison and not sustain life but threaten it. The tipping point is when we indulge in sense pleasures, become numb, and lose ourselves. When that happens, we forget the purpose of life and our important vocations, such as self-reflection and the inner work of developing courage and compassion.

People may be attached to social status, fame, and wealth—none of which are crucial for survival. What this attachment does is to make us worship and seek meaning from them. We then shut the door to an interior life, the possibility of discovering who we truly are. The higher purpose of life becomes remote. We are fooled by a false sense of happiness, and the path to true happiness is obscured by our dependence on external conditions. We anxiously hold tight to them and are afraid of losing them. The intoxication of status, fame, and wealth shuts down meaningful inquiry into the real root of suffering. To get at this obstacle and root it out, some yogis give away all their possessions and any wealth they may have. Their practice becomes a life of simplicity, without the usual comforts, so that they can experience real freedom.

There are many stories about spiritual teachers giving away their belongings as a radical way to let go of attachment. However, it is not important whether or not we literally abandon possessions, status, money, and comfort, since there is nothing wrong with them in themselves. It is the obsession and attachment to them that binds us. Conversely, we could have all the riches in the world and also have ultimate freedom from spiritual and psychological obscurations by abiding in a state of inner equanimity, no longer seduced by external conditions. The whole intention of the path is not to become a holy hobo but to overcome the attachment itself.

Our relationship to the conventional world can become an emblem of attachment when it becomes a comfort zone, providing ego with a solid sense of self and security. This "self" feels like it has ground under its feet. Modern conveniences—such as grocery stores, cars, social media, air conditioning, and sensual comforts—contribute to the illusion. In many ways the modern world is wild because it amplifies such attachment through ideals of materialism, capitalism, and meritocracy, encouraging people to strive to be special, famous, or rich. This was not true in most indigenous cultures. Our society worships famous people: movie stars, writers, dancers, chefs, yoga instructors, reality TV personalities, and even spiritual teachers. But fame is like a water bubble, with no real substance or deep inquiry, created only by advertisements, social media, and appeals to mass instincts. Social media plays an important role in this illusion. Many people believe in their bubble of fame and become tormented by the unhealthy desire to maintain it. Others are tormented by their desire to become special or famous. We have lost discernment between what is real and valuable, between what holds merit and what is a bunch of bologna.

People are often challenged by the idea of letting go of attachment to sense pleasures, called *döyön* in Tibetan. This term refers to desirable sense objects and any desired qualities that please the five senses. The teaching to let go of these may be interpreted as an outdated asceticism or puritanical ideology. But to clarify, letting go of attachment to sense pleasures is not the same as stating that there is something intrinsically wrong with them. They play an important part in human life. They are among the things that make life magical and directly connect us with reality. Sometimes pleasures can be simple, not debauched or hedonistic, like walking on the beach with bare feet or eating delicious food that your mother used to cook when you had a cold. Padampa is not rejecting these simple enjoyments. He is saying that we should not be lost in debauchery or sense pleasures, because it makes us lose our dignity and integrity and eventually corrupts us. Fame and wealth likewise are not bad in themselves but can lead to this same end.

In this context, attachment can be very subtle, referring not only to physical things but also to our concepts, ideas, and belief systems. In some sense, cutting through attachment to concepts is more challenging than letting go of attachment to physical things. Concepts often serve to give the illusion of a framework for our relationship to reality. They seem to provide a sense of right and wrong and a way to understand how the world is constructed. In this way, attachment to concepts becomes a powerful obstacle to inner freedom.

Taking refuge in the three jewels—Buddha, Dharma, and Sangha—is one of the most sacred aspects of Buddhist practice. But even our reverence for them can become a trap of ego, and eventually we should transcend attachment to them as well. This is why the Mahayana tradition regards the Buddha as the Dharmakaya Buddha—unborn and unconditioned. Dharmakaya Buddha has no form, no characteristics, and is the true Buddha. There is nothing left to be attached to. In the same way, Buddhism even encourages letting go of attachment to enlightenment as a goal of spiritual striving. Shantideva said that the idea of fruition is useful in the beginning because it inspires people to begin the spiritual path. But in the end, he said that believing there is something to attain is a form of ignorance.

Even the sacred can sometimes be a trap of ego and become an obstacle for true inner liberation. This is also taught in the Dzogchen teachings on the nature mind, such as those by Longchenpa, who said that our consciousness can be tied in metal chains or golden chains. The metal chains are attachments to ordinary things in life—possessions and negative states of mind. Golden chains are attachments to spiritual experiences, notions of the sacred, and enlightenment. Even extraordinary ideals, such as being a bodhisattva and helping all beings, can be traps if we are attached to them. Such ideals are sublime and inspiring, but if we become attached to them as the virtue of all virtues, they are just another trap.

At the same time as we seek enlightenment, we are transcending conceptual attachment to it. Attachment to the notion of enlightenment is another way of reifying the duality that is a false version of reality. Paradoxically, enlightenment itself is free of all attachment. Attachment to physical objects is easier to recognize, because we can see, feel, and taste their physical form and viscerally experience our attachment to them. But clinging to mental objects, such as belief systems, is more difficult to recognize. They are not "things" that we can get rid of or see easily, yet they shape our entire view of reality. We may not know we are even attached to them. Concepts veil our minds, obscuring our ability to distinguish between the nature of reality and the concepts themselves. They become the lens through which we see reality. This is why we do not dare challenge them. The world seems to be the way we think it is. Our concepts seem to be true and valid. Very quickly, we elevate them into sacred truths. One thing leads to another: once our concepts seem real, ego begins to construct a conditioned reality around it, building one seeming truth upon another. Buddhist teachings say that there is no strategizing or negotiating—one must let go of attachment to get to enlightenment. Beyond attachment is unprecedented freedom and joy, which ego was not counting on.

Traveling into unknown, wild places—in the world and in our minds—is an essential practice in Tantric Buddhism, especially Chöd. The sixth axiom is the topic of the next chapter, "Journey into the Haunted Ground."

7. REALIZE MIND LIKE SKY

This axiom is an invitation to realize the nature of mind. This principle transcends doctrinal differences between Tibetan lineages, as all of them include this cornerstone Mahayana teaching. The nature of mind is the ultimate truth to which we can awaken. It can be experienced through contemplation and meditation. It is not a supernatural entity outside of yourself but is the unconditioned state of consciousness. The yogi or meditator should turn attention inward to seek absolute freedom—the divine buddha nature—and to find the highest liberation. In doing so, this radical insight arises that everything you are searching for is within you. You see that the very nature of mind is what you have been searching for. This is what it means when Buddhist masters say, "Buddha is within."

The nature of mind is often referred to as "original mind." This does not mean everyday-life mind, superficial small mind, intoxicated by ego's countless illusions and delusions. Original mind is already free, not bound by our thoughts, opinions, ideas, or beliefs. Therefore, it is not only free but has natural equilibrium and joy. This is uplifting news, because it immediately conjures a state of mind that is freeing, boundless, and replete with natural awakening. It is always present in us.

On one hand, we are stuck in small ego-based mind, continuously feeding the mental habits that fuel the vicious circle of suffering. On the other hand, we long for an enlightened state of consciousness where all limitations to reality are transcended. This longing is why people are drawn to spiritual disciplines, such as meditation and rituals. We are torn between these diametric desires of protecting and cherishing a separate self and longing for ultimate and boundless spiritual freedom. The sixth Dalai Lama, Tsangyang Gyatso says in his love poems:

My mind is drawn toward my lover.
If my mind were as drawn to Dharma as this,
in this very body, in this very life,
buddhahood would be attained.

Generally, human beings are not one hundred percent spiritual. We are both spiritual and mundane. Parts of us want to continue to be finite while other parts long to become infinite. Theoretically, if our longing to be infinite is stronger than our ordinary desires, then enlightenment is supposed to be an easy feat. But our mind is often in default mode. We fall prey to animal-istic urges, even at the cost of others' well-being. Through that, we are trapped in ruthless dog-eat-dog thinking, which views other human beings as competitors. Though this trap causes so much suffering, there is a simultaneous natural urge driving us to seek transcendence.

As a generalization, the main difference between religious and spiritual people is that religious people tend to look for tran-scendence from outside, through their relationship to the divine, whereas many spiritual people in today's world tend to seek tran-scendence through exploring their own consciousness. In general, the spiritual person may find that human life has limitations, such as hatred, love, despising our enemies, favoring our friends, hope for success, fear of failure, and being shackled by conventions. Yet, the spiritual person may suspect that these are not built on truth but on illusion. They recognize that these hindrances can be tran-scended by changing their consciousness. Often, they may become committed to a spiritual path of meditation and begin to have a direct glimpse of extraordinary freedom, experiencing boundless compassion, joy, and selflessness. They often come across a deep understanding that such experiences are not an altered state of mind but are in fact the very nature of mind, like returning home. This is often described as being like sky, because it is the best anal-ogy for what is vast, spacious, unhindered, limitless, and impartial. Sometimes people have a glimpse of this in ordinary moments, not just while meditating or engaging in spiritual practice. This is not unusual, because they are simply in touch with the pure nature of the mind.

The feeling of transcendence can occur during powerful life experiences or even through taking mind altering substances like hallucinogens. These experiences, though induced, perhaps allow a glimpse of the state beyond mundane mind. For example, I read in *The New Yorker* of a situation where doctors used alternative methods to alleviate the pain of a man diagnosed with terminal cancer. They created a positive ambiance with sacred images and gave him hallucinogens. He became very happy and was infused with positive feelings. He even felt that his cancer cells were beautiful. His wife later said that the last few months of his life were very loving due to this treatment. The traditional masters always say that true nature of mind is not an altered state and that the most direct entry into the nature of mind is to not do anything, to not manipulate consciousness in any way. What this man experienced may not have been exactly the nature of mind, but it was possibly a glimpse into a state beyond mundane mind.

The teaching of "mind like sky" resonates with the spiritual impulse, even at a theoretical level. It feels so desirable that there is a limitless state—free of neuroses, envy, anxiety, with all pressures gone. Yet, "mind like sky" is not an altered state of mind or super consciousness that belongs only to deities. Instead, it is the closest thing to you—that is why it is the *nature* of mind. Such an epiphany can happen spontaneously, in a flash, or through a sudden catalytic event. This sudden realization can dawn through illness, tragedy, one of life's dramas, beautiful music, poetry, spiritual verses, or even something mundane. Anything can cause a sudden opening into vast awareness, freedom from conditions, where we are no longer operating from ego-based consciousness. We simply have to notice when it occurs.

Ancient masters encouraged silent retreat as an invitation to profound insight. Dropping daily chores and mundane activities and simply resting in silence often reveals innate openness. When we devote time to simplicity and silence, the mundane, busy mind that was there disappears like clouds dissolving in the sky, and the natural state is revealed. It is totally free and spacious, not bound by thoughts or moods. Anxiety, doubt, story lines, and emotional context dissolve on the spot. Silence and solitude often invite this epiphany.

Through meditation practice, profound glimpses can happen again and again. Discernment grows, and we see—like the difference between day and night—the difference between living in ordinary life and in non-egoic sky-like mind. It is like the difference between living in a little cell versus living in a royal palace. Through meditation and through our commitment to bring this experience into everyday life, our mind becomes more and more attuned to it. As a result, we begin to live life from that state of mind rather than the egoic mind, which causes so much suffering. Therefore, the more we practice, the more we can abide in awakened mind.

The idea that mind is like sky is a hard concept to buy. The mind we are most familiar with does not fit this picture. Buddhist teachings often leave the impression that to have such an experience, we must work for years and years, carving away at inner obstacles, finally arriving at the moment when mental obstacles dissolve. Many Buddhist folk tales and traditional stories speak of this long-strived-for moment of awakening—this hard-earned perfect moment. Yet, the nature of mind is actually quite accessible. It can be immediately and spontaneously realized. To our common understanding, the nature of mind may seem a bit mystical, because in our daily experience the ordinary thinking mind, which is run by ego, seems like the foundation of mind. Within this conditioned egoic mind, it is not always clear how we are suffering. Sometimes suffering happens at a subconscious level, triggering emotional contraction. Often there are tiny thoughts happening that can have a clandestine power to dampen our life force. When this occurs, we are not able to love, forgive, or transcend as much as we want to. These forces, though, are like clouds in the sky. They are not concrete. They are nonmaterial mental formations and can therefore dissolve. Those moments when they dissolve—when we gracefully fall into mind beyond ego, free from its confines—reveal the mind to be just like the sky.

———

These seven axioms are usually recounted in Machig Labdrön's biography as distilling the whole body of Buddhist teachings. Because of that, understanding them requires a commentary to unpack their deeper meaning. In preparation for this book, I went back to other Chöd writings and liturgies for more understanding, but so far I have not come across any single authoritative commentary on these aphorisms. They are so richly nuanced that there are many ways of interpreting them. But what is clear is that they are not only profound but extremely radical. They are for those who have the guts to be honest with themselves and the willingness to challenge themselves. The direct message of these teachings is critical for inner awakening, whether we like it or not. They are not just spiritual Band-Aids or palliative steps but serve as an invitation to be on a serious path that requires complete dedication.

2

Journey into the Haunted Ground

The crux of Chöd practice is our journey into the haunted ground. This journey is the sixth of the seven key instructions imparted to Machig Labdrön by Padampa Sangye discussed in the previous chapter. In Tibetan, the term *nyensa*, or "haunted ground," means a place that is haunted by demons and spirits, where lost souls wander. It describes any place that provokes inner fear and anxiety, but it is traditionally a term used for cemeteries. The cemeteries in Tibet are often used as a haunted ground where individuals go to do this practice, partly because they are unsettling for Tibetan people. People go there to practice in order to intentionally invoke all sorts of neuroses, because the uncomfortable nature of the environment makes is easier for them to bring up their inner demons, mainly fear. What they are really trying to invoke is the demon of reification—making things more real in our minds than they are. Our minds can make something out of nothing and make us prone to losing track of reality. Reification is like the father or mother neurosis, giving rise to all neuroses. For example, by inquiring into the nature of fear, we see that it often boils down to reification. We take the objects of fear, such as the demons in a cemetery, to be more real than they are.

In that sense, a haunted ground can be a literal place, like a cemetery or Canyon de Chelly, but it can also be a metaphor for a state of consciousness where our conflicting emotions lie. These emotions bind us in confusion and obscure the nature of reality. Being in such a physical place outside of our comfort zones, with the right intentions, we easily become more conscious of our usual neuroses and can get into the more hidden realms of our psyche to meet the more devious demons. On the other hand, haunted ground is everywhere, because we can meet our inner demons wherever we are. Our identification with inner demons can be severed by meeting them face to face. Otherwise, they continuously live hidden in us, ruling our lives without knowing. This practice of meeting inner demons face to face could be regarded as a radical form of developing self-knowledge. Without radical self-knowledge, our spiritual practice can become a form of entertainment for our egos, a subtle self-deception in which we have the illusion of being spiritual while actually being under the control of conflicting emotions.

I jokingly suggested once to a Chöd retreat group that the forty of us go to Europe together and make a Chöd pilgrimage along the Camino de Santiago trail. The Camino de Santiago is a large network of ancient pilgrimage routes, on which many people in Europe have experienced a powerful shift in consciousness. It seemed ideal to be able to make such a journey and, on the way, also visit beautiful villages and eat delicious bread and cheese! Another time, a group of us went to France and stayed at a property owned by friends. It was an old chateau that was well past its days of glory but still impressive. One of the many rooms in it was a dungeon, where perhaps lots of people had been in captivity. One courageous friend decided to sleep in the dungeon, to welcome whatever fear she wanted to work with. The dungeon was like her haunted ground. But, while we might mistakenly imagine that the haunted ground is only the uncomfortable, scary environments we have visited, many masters brilliantly teach that everywhere is haunted ground. Life is haunted ground wherever we go. Life is run by inner demons until we have pacified them.

Going to the haunted ground is more than just working with our usual psychological stuff. The journey is delving into all aspects of consciousness, inviting upheaval so that we can meet inner demons in our own psyche. In Tibetan, this upheaval or uprising is referred to as *lhongtsé*, which means deliberately provoking inner conflicting emotions from the dark recesses of your consciousness. It brings you face to face with your inner demons, which presents the opportunity to let go of identification with them on the spot.

A journey into unknown wild places, whether internal or external, is a powerful endeavor for spiritual awakening. Such a journey speedily ripens the effects of spiritual practice. But if you are not properly prepared for this powerful, radical approach, unintended consequences can emerge. You can be thrown off balance with overwhelming internal upheavals that can shake you to the core. Such a situation can be tricky to handle. For this reason, people in Tibet do not just pick up a book on Chöd and start doing it. They seek out an authentic lama who is well trained and then receive instructions from them. For centuries, this student-teacher relationship has been the guiding light of Chöd, ensuring that the student understands the true meaning of what they are undertaking. In Tibet, it has always been practiced this way for the safety and sanity of the practitioner.

Many Tibetans are afraid of the demons who are said to inhabit haunted places. There are many stories of cemeteries filled with demons who emerge from the sleeping world in the evening and remain hidden during the day. These are often spoken of as the wandering spirits of dead people or as demons stuck for centuries in pain. It is said that these spirits seek to bring humans into their own misery. For many Tibetans, this ethereal world is not separate from the everyday world of form. It is not mythical but as real as anything else—as real as people, or the highway, or their living room furniture. This may be why Machig Labdrön emphatically talked of demons as part of our state of mind—because she was teaching Tibetan disciples who viewed reality this way. Not only that, she skillfully used demons as symbolic representations of our neuroses, which made it easier for people to clarify what those neuroses are and see them clearly.

This perception of cemetery dwellers as real beings is perhaps universal. Though landscaped like gardens, cemeteries in the Western world are still places of fear for some people, and many cultures share the idea of wandering, disembodied occupants of graveyards. One of the most powerful teachings of Chöd is to realize that demons are mental projections and not get scared or run away from them but see them clearly as forces in our own psyches. As Lama Yakwang instructed me when I was a young person, by staying in nondual awareness, we are protected from them. The practice emphasizes staying with them until the journey is complete. No matter what level of fear or what monstrous visions arise, we should see the visions as a figment of imagination and not give life to them. The journey ends when this fear has been conquered or the demon of reification is under our control.

For some who fear cemeteries, making the journey there and returning from it is an authentic way to conquer deep fear. But to others, going to a cemetery or spending the night there is not a heroic journey at all. These people have other places that scare them. Many people in the West are tormented by phobias and can appreciate this journey from that point of view. Some therapies suggest that if a person is afraid of spiders, they should go to a place filled with spiders to look into the nature of their phobia and come out of it having conquered the fear. Or if they are afraid of heights, they should go to high places. In the end, fear comes from our tendency to reify the thing that we are afraid of, and this is true for all other neuroses as well. Once we directly encounter the source of our fear and see it for all its complexity, we no longer reify it, or see it as a solid real thing, and so we no longer fear it.

There are stories in Tibet of people teasing Chödpas practicing in the charnel ground by dressing up as demons, holding burning torches, and making terrifying noises in the dark. Some Chödpas became so frightened that they ran away without having time to pack their ritual instruments. These stories might have been true but later became like folklore told as entertainment around dinner. Either way, this shows that even for some Chödpas, fear and expectation are the most powerful emotions that rule our lives, and Chöd is about cutting the very root of them. They bind us in the chain of suffering. If we are no longer bound by fear, what replaces it is love and joy. The process is to first become friendly with that fear and then continue to reveal our more subtle identification with it.

Our fears, hang-ups, addictions, jealousy, pride, resistance, and illusions continually rule us. We are aware of some of these dark forces but not of many others. Some people might feel these forces in their daily life but not have the sense that they are problems. This is a form of ignorance. With this ignorance, there is little hope for change. If we become aware of these forces, we become comfortable with them and let them become like building blocks for our sense of self. In this way, we do not need a strong intention to confront them directly or pacify them. Rather, awareness gives us the power to energetically cut through the cord of identifying with them.

Traditionally, Chödpas travel around, sometimes staying in many different locations on their journey. With simple supplies and by living in inhospitable places, they aspire to have a powerful life-changing shift in consciousness. Many conquer their inner darkness and have significant awakening to the nature of reality. Such a journey, though challenging, can sound very romantic. This is not just a Chöd concept, but a universal truth in many traditions. When life demands change because we are not thriving or have fallen prey to destructive habits, we might hear an inner wake-up call. This may be a strong desire to leave our familiar environment, to leave civilization, to change diet and lifestyle, to get out of a place full of unhealthy habits, and to seek refuge in the purity and serenity of the natural world. People across cultures go on soul journeys to purify and cleanse and for inner transformation.

By journeying into the wilderness alone, walking trails with few footprints and very little sign of human civilization, where animals roam freely, the knots of unhealthy habits can naturally unravel. When done with the aspiration to change, going into solitude opens the possibility of deep insight, like a rebirth. Cheryl Strayed's book *Wild* tells her story of hiking the Pacific Crest Trail. Addicted to drugs, her life in shambles, she began the trek to come to know her true self and reclaim her life. Something internal inspired her to stop and to radically uproot her habits. She decided to pack food and clothes and hike this trail, to walk it alone until she felt healed. This is an extraordinary example of how we can let go and cut through unhealthy energetic patterns by being in nature on a pilgrimage.

Living in solitude in nature is much-needed medicine. Most parts of the world have become a screen culture, with people disconnected from each other, living in a concrete jungle. Our world has become a virtual reality. I see lots of unhappiness among the younger generation especially. This cut-off cultural comfort zone is not serving our best interests. People forget how healing it can be to reconnect with nature and with our humanity. Once we are out of the familiar, there is space to truly realize who we are, what life is all about, and what matters most to us. We see that we have been a prisoner to the conventions of the world. Lots of the old emotions fester in us like unhealed wounds, but in the haunted ground when old emotions and unhealed wounds show up, they are ready for complete healing. We do not have to let them haunt us forever or keep us from living fully. The natural world is a nonjudgmental cosmic mother and makes us feel safe to feel pain without fear, without the need to hide anything. It is like nature is gently saying, "You are free to fall apart."

THE HAUNTED GROUND OF SOCIETY

The natural world is friendly and provides us with the bounty of sunlight, water, resources, food, crops, and medicine. And at the same time, it can be extremely uncooperative. Nature has a harsh side, which can threaten our existence. Many species (ours included) form great networks to sustain and protect their existence. This network is the very thing that defines society. Humanity has survived by forming societies, large and small, from local indigenous tribes in the Amazon jungle to powerful nations filled with riches and sophisticated art, music, military, and innovation. Without social networks, no one can survive easily. Society is necessary for our individual and collective survival. Yet, it does not always work in our favor.

Society is like a complex, many-dimensioned being with a life of its own. It is born naturally through the instincts of people to gather together to work to sustain our existence. This complex being then becomes so powerful that it begins to rule us, and it is difficult to go against it. Everyone is bound by its structure, its social norms. And in the face of these, individuals often give up their own minds and aspirations. Blinded by trends and social pressure, we may lose sight of what is right and wrong and may go along like sheep with a distasteful value system.

It is not as if this social haunted ground has a single shepherd that moves people along with the trends and collective values that easily sweep us up. When everyone around us—neighbors, cousins, and nieces—become part of it, few individuals can maintain their insight or enlightened values. We become trapped by the demon of ignorance, losing our awareness to the collective mindset. Throughout history, some of humanity's great thinkers and bright souls have broken the spell and demonstrated awakening, like the Buddha. Often shunned and misunderstood, they have shown a compassionate and radical way to live. Their eyes are open to the nature of reality. But for most people in everyday life, the demons of competition, judgement, aggression, and comparison create a society that is a haunted ground. When we look inside, whenever we interact, some of these demons become active. Conventional society does not usually train people to work with each other from the ground of open heart and true kindness.

Sometimes, in simple social situations, such as going out with a group of people, we find ourselves trying to be funny or feeling jealous of someone with better looks, more money, or more charisma. Sometimes going along with social conventions is painful, especially if we are pulled into behavior and states of mind unconsciously. There is an unspoken influence when we gather in groups, subjecting us to these social games, trapping us in the bondage of complicated relations. Religious societies are not exempt; they have their own conventions different from those of lay people.

There can be a dark side to religious societies. Chöd is considered the path of radical observance because it has an element of countering or discarding both worldly and religious conventions. Chöd is the perfect antidote to the religious conventions that bind us and are actually based on unenlightened principles.

Even if we are encouraged by Buddhist masters to go into deep retreat, in the end we must come back to the world. The ancient yogis did deep practice away from the world, taking a break from society to experience freedom from social bondage. The point is not to run away from people but to investigate ourselves and see the inner demons that show up around others and then learn to rise above them by not following or being subject to them. We can choose to see them and not get lost in them. Though some people take refuge in isolation, often because they are fed up with humanity, this can become just a spiritual hideout. There are all sorts of ways to avoid the discomfort of social haunted-ground demons, because it is true that some of these inner demons do not come out when you are not around people. But authentic growth actually comes to fruition in relation to people. In the absence of challenge, how do you know what it is to forgive? If you do not witness the suffering of others, how do you know what true compassion is? How do you know true love if you do not engage with meaningful relationships?

———

In modern culture, careers often form the basis for how we define ourselves within society. Here, the inner demons of ambition and identity can lead to losing contact with fundamental human kindness and forgetting the higher purpose of life. Some professionals become like a beast willing to do anything to climb to the top of the ladder. People can become mesmerized by the spell of ambition. It is a palpable atmosphere in many modern professional environments. It happens everywhere: universities, hospitals, tech companies, and corporate offices.

I was once invited to teach a course on *The Way of the Bodhisattva*, a Buddhist classic written by the eighth-century monk Shantideva, for a Buddhist club at a famous tech company. This is a Mahayana text on cultivating the mind of enlightenment, and I accepted the invitation to teach it. I had always thought that people who worked at that company would be very lucky and happy. I imagined that there would be a sense of glory in working there. It is such a famous company, whose name is a household word in many parts of the world. Tourists from all over the world travel to stand in front of their sign and take selfies. The campus is well manicured, the offices are impressive, and the cafeteria is filled with all types of delicious food. Most of the workers are young and seem to be optimistic. However, as I got to know the participants in the Buddhist group, I was told that there was a lot of unhappiness among the workers, which burst my bubble.

Employees are hired there because of their exceptional academic histories and because they are outstanding performers in many ways. They are accomplished and smart. Yet, as I spent time getting to know them, and being in the corporate headquarters, I began to hear how many of them desperately wanted to be special, how driven they were by ambition, and how competitively they wanted to advance in the company. But many do not become part of the elite. When they do not get the raise or promotion, their identity as a top performer is damaged, which leads some to disappointment and depression. That is the haunted ground of career: the demon of ambition, of materialism, of heartlessness roaming around wildly.

This phenomenon has developed within the last two centuries. Our modern world created unprecedented conveniences, opportunities, possibilities, comforts, and luxuries in abundance. The choices kept growing as time went by. In the old days, most people lived quite simply. If you were a farmer or nomad, life was simple. People did not have many opportunities for education and college degrees, to chase their dreams and plan for a career. There were limited opportunities to be a successful artist or entrepreneur. Now, the list of possibilities is unending. Today, even average citizens in developed countries like the United States have comforts and luxuries that the great emperors of Rome or the Mongolian empires could not even imagine for themselves. I once read an interview with a man who stated that everyone makes six figures in his neighborhood. He said that his neighbors had more comforts and conveniences than the early dynasty of the Rockefellers during the Gilded Age. Back then, there were no televisions with endless channels or excesses of exotic foods available to everyone. Humanity has never enjoyed this level of physical well-being now available.

Though the world may be in a golden era, the progress comes with a heavy price: the wounds in our psyches. The result is broken family structures, loss of connection with ancestors, and a plague of isolation and unhappiness. Outwardly, our society is suffering from unchecked, unleashed individualism and competition. The illusion of meritocracy mesmerizes us into thinking that we can chase our dreams, get a lucrative career, and achieve glory. Yet, the harsh continual competitiveness and stark comparisons to others leaves us feeling left behind, jealous, and deficient. Desire for recognition, advancement, fame, achievement, and money infiltrate careers, causing suffering and confusion. Employees are rewarded for these same things. These golden handcuffs bind career professionals. Seduced by external rewards, they may find it almost impossible to delve into inner meaning and bring haunted ground demons to light. Remaining committed to uprooting inner poisons can liberate them even in the haunted ground of career. Bringing the light of awareness to the demons that emerge in this context makes it possible to use them as the very force for transformation. In this way, careers and other societal markers of identity are not intrinsically detrimental to the spiritual path, but in fact their challenges can become the very ground from which inner demons are cut through.

THE HAUNTED GROUND OF RELATIONSHIP

In the region of Kongpo in Tibet, a respected Chödpa was once asked if he had ever done a journey into the haunted ground of the cemetery. He said "No, I haven't gone. I don't need to go because I'm married." Within the haunted ground of relationship, many old neurotic patterns get triggered. We develop habits of dumping emotional baggage on our partners, triggering reactions that ricochet back on us. When we are blind to our own demons of jealousy, complaint, paranoia, and dissatisfaction, these unresolved shadowy patterns are easily projected on the other. But they are the demons of our own unfinished issues. Some people continue to place blame on the relationship and the partner and move from one connection to another, thinking they will find a perfect companion with whom no problems will emerge. If we do not look inside and recognize our own confusion, each new relationship will trigger the same old upheavals.

Human relationships seem to have been composed of the same dynamics from time immemorial. For eons, human relationships have been tied to personal desire, expectations, value systems, and religion. In some cultures, until recently, intimate relationships were thought to be only between a man and a woman, and these were often arranged by parents or community. Committed relationships were not always based on finding a soul mate, romantic passion, or falling in love at first sight. It was often required that the family know the background and heritage of the partner and bless the union. Romantic love is a fairly recent social behavior. Over the course of human history, this approach accounts for very little of humanity's time here. Yet, in the unconscious and in fairy tales the mythology of love says we can find the perfect mate, someone who unconditionally loves your smells, has a magical connection to you, will live forever, and will raise a family with you. This is part of the relationship neuroses of the modern world. It is based on people not understanding what love is.

The term "love" is used indiscriminately from romantic comedies to tragic and dangerous liaisons. It is a romantic concept created by the Western world. In other cultures, people will sing in their own language but still use the English phrase "I love you" embedded in the song. The phrase is an enticing illusion but inevitably leads to coming back to a more realistic and ordinary place, sometimes resulting in disillusionment. This can be seen as positive, as a cute illusion, and someone might ask me, "Why don't you just let people enjoy it? Why burst the bubble?" But the mythology will exceed what life delivers, and no one can really fulfill the expectations of love. At the outset of a relationship, people try to be on their best behavior. But no one can act forever, and eventually who we really are surfaces. Our weaknesses and unfinished business join the party.

As we begin dumping psychological garbage, and our partner does the same, there is disharmony, blaming, and painful separation. False illusions of a soul mate, jealousy, and the desire to control make partners become aloof or grasping, unleashing deep disappointment. Within the stress of trying to maintain an idealized romance, partners can become possessive of each other, and the whole enterprise of passion can change from sweet to bitter. Though people feel they love each other, they do not really know what this means. Love may turn into hatred or resentment. Modern society needs to be reeducated as to what love is and to get a clear definition of what it is. Otherwise, carnal passion, erotic impulses, and fantasies are mistaken for love.

As time goes by, all kinds of problems can develop in a relationship and cause the illusion to collapse: for example, aloofness, boredom, gaslighting, and manipulation. These strategies are inner demons that tend to lurk in relationships unless we intentionally uncover them, own them, and start working on them. By working through them, relationships can be a source of happiness and can even allow us to find authentic joy from learning what true love is in its deepest meaning. Authentic love is to understand both strengths and weaknesses, of yourself and others, and accept them all. It is a dynamic dance of give and take without conditions, of letting go into uncertainty and vulnerability, and being willing to help that person when needed.

It is unfortunate that pain accompanies the breakdown of the romantic myth, but this is exactly why relationships can be regarded as another productive haunted ground. Some believe that if we aspire to truly grow spiritually, we should be in a relationship and have children. Seeing our inner demons reflected in the mirror of intimate connection and nuclear or extended family life, we are forced to mature and learn what it means to become truly selfless and to know what it means to love another human being more than ourselves. Maybe the true doorway to enlightenment is not escaping into a meditation cave but is raising a family.

One day, while leading a meditation retreat in the artist community of Mendocino, California, a woman approached me in the greeting line after my talk. She described a painful situation with her partner, who abused her emotionally. Mendocino is like a fairytale village. Its Pacific redwoods on high cliffs above the ocean and quaint historic buildings make it feel like a bit of heaven. I love to go there, not just to lead meditation retreats but also to drive along Highway 1 and revel in the ocean scenery. While I had been blissed out from the heavenly quality of the town, the woman's story reminded me that I was still in the human world.

In listening to her and taking in her distress, I could not say to her, "Oh, let go of your pain." When I asked how long ago this relationship had happened, she said it had been many years. So, I said, "Maybe you can find peace. Find a picture of your partner to express all your anger to and then burn it. Then you may find peace." She relaxed and smiled after hearing this. Her haunted ground was holding on to her anger for so long. By making conscious that she was holding on to something that was no longer part of her life, she could stop abusing herself with the memory. Even when emotions have merit, even when abusers die, we internalize them and end up abusing ourselves and making ourselves miserable. The time comes to let go. This is not to say that we should suppress our feelings. Emotional pain caused by others tends to linger in us because many people do not honor the pain or fully express it. Expressing pain is perhaps the first step toward healing, and each person must find their own way to do it.

Transcending self is a grand concept. The question is how we can experience this in an authentic way. People can experience this by raising children or taking care of elderly parents or friends. Giving up sleep and vacations, giving up money and happiness, and foregoing their own needs is a path to spiritual growth. Fulfilling the true commitment of a relationship is extraordinary, unrelenting selfless activity. It is one of the most authentic ways that humanity can experience self-transcendence. This is authentic selflessness, not the endorphin-intoxicated spiritual trance that some mistakenly think of as the transcendent experience.

A common fantasy about spirituality is that it is a grace-filled, benevolent journey where everything is holy. Many people gravitate to spiritual practice to find peace and a higher state of consciousness, but spirituality in itself is a complicated and complex world where wild things can happen. It is a haunted ground filled with inner demons that might include pride, denial, delusion, and pretense. Spiritual escapism, for example, is nothing more than yet another inner deception. By persistently chasing a state of bliss, we can be left with all of our neuroses while we tell ourselves a fantastic story that we are getting somewhere. It would be like a homeowner covering their filthy floor with a rug rather than cleaning it. The bad odor underneath will eventually start to come out and permeate the atmosphere. The owner may have grown used to it, becoming oblivious, but others will certainly notice that something is foul.

Spirituality is not pure and hunky-dory like we think it is supposed to be. It is not an obvious, straight, or absolute path strewn with flowers like we might imagine. It is messy and tricky. One part of the dark side of spirituality is that it comes with a throng of delusions that can be harder to dismantle than those in the secular world, precisely because they are held as sacred. The demons of fundamentalism, dogma, mindless discipline, and self-importance are rife in spiritual practices. They are difficult to let go of because we conflate them with being spiritual. We can be bound by these invisible golden chains that foster a sense of duality rather than transcendence. If we practice without recognizing this propensity, we might just be indulging our compulsions.

I visited an ancient world heritage site temple in Korea in 2019 called Daeheungsa and was struck by its timeless sacredness. As we entered this extraordinary site, we were drawn forward by its ancient charm, but the divine wrathful guardian carved above the entry gate stopped us in our tracks. One of the nuns in our group told us that some people are afraid to go through the gate because of these demon guardians. This was a significant metaphor, telling us that the spiritual path would not always be beautiful and wholesome, where we do not have to dig up our neuroses. It was also a reminder that true spirituality demands that we let go of the illusions that we are so attached to.

There are many Buddhist masters who seem quite blank from having deconstructed all the ideas they held about themselves and others. One time a famous lama wrote beautiful hymns of praise to the Tibetan master, Patrul Rinpoche. When Patrul Rinpoche read them, he left and did not come back for days, as though it was too much praise for him or as if it shocked him. No one knew where he went. It is not that he did not live up to the hymns, but he was cautious about people possibly getting attached to their grand illusions about him. He did not want to buy into grand illusions about himself either. His leaving was a powerful teaching to everyone, because there was no longer anyone there to project their illusions onto. It was like taking a movie screen away from a movie projector.

Another spiritual shadow is when some wealthy Buddhist patrons do not really want to practice real spirituality, compassion, love, or self-reflection because they believe that money will help them gain merit without doing the real work. The story they tell themselves is that you can buy anything if you have enough money: merit, good karma, enlightenment, and so on. So they give money to monasteries and to famous teachers. They can boast that it all looks good from the outside. They fool themselves into thinking they are on the right path and that enlightenment will come knocking on their door at any moment, all without having to challenge their ego-clinging. Some part of them truly does want to have good karma, but it is all tied up in this shadow.

A similar illustration of self-centered, ulterior-motivated generosity is the story of the Indian king Prasenajit. This king had great wealth and invited the Buddha with his students to dine at his palace for several months. He offered his noble guests food and shelter. A beggar woman saw that the Buddha and his disciples were there, and she came each day to practice with them outside the palace grounds. She viewed the king's generosity and great wealth as a testament to his having accumulated great merit, and she rejoiced in what he was doing.

At day's end, when it was time to dedicate the merit, the Buddha asked King Prasenajit, "Would you like me to dedicate the source of merit that you have acquired to you, or shall I dedicate it to someone who is more worthy of it than you?" The king instructed the Buddha to dedicate it to whomever had the greatest source of merit. Buddha dedicated the merit to the beggar woman outside the palace grounds. Each evening, the king made this same request and the Buddha gave the same response, until the jealous king finally devised a way to punish the beggars assembled outside. He tricked the beggars into gathering to eat food spilled on the ground by his ministers, but then had the ministers beat the beggars away. The king's ulterior motives negated his merit, but the beggars' pure motivation was profound.

Even closely held spiritual community, our relationships with spiritual brothers and sisters, can be considered haunted ground territory. Spiritual community is paradoxical, because it is supposed to be holy, pure or at least noble, and to consist of beautiful beings on a noble path. Inner demons can take root in the community consciousness and begin to dominate it. People often enter a relationship with a spiritual community with their own projections in full force. Their hopes and aspirations of what may be gained from it, as well as the projections laid on them as they enter, can be challenging. Facing these projections can lead to a sense of disappointment and separateness.

It is healthy for people to realize that spiritual communities have their own shadow. Such a realization helps people to not have such high, unrealistic projections about the community, which could lead to unwholesome consequences. People who are part of these communities are human beings who have their own complex personalities. Sometimes, both leaders and followers in spiritual communities can act out their shadow, which has unfortunate outcomes and pain for everyone. If we view spiritual community as haunted ground and use the wisdom of this view in the beginning, it will help to not fall into unwholesome traps. Haunted ground may seem to be the opposite of what we believe a spiritual community is, but it is where the demons of pride, delusion, sectarianism, and unreasonable expectations are always lurking.

Once the shadow side of spirituality is brought into awareness through mindfulness and awareness, we can immediately see our consciousness begin to evolve. Others can witness it as well. Self-reflection becomes the most rewarding and joyous work you can do in life. It is not like you are doing this work only for yourself; others are impacted by it as well. Other people will also benefit because you exude more love. You will naturally refrain from causing them pain. Then, whatever is done by one person has a ripple effect on the collective consciousness. Even though we cannot measure this with data, intuitive wisdom and experience speak this truth. We are part of the world, and the world is part of us.

THE HAUNTED GROUND OF SHADOW

I have used the word *shadow* in this chapter in a way that is somewhat related to the shadow that is talked about in psychology. The word in this context means both spiritual obstruction and anything that can block natural awakening. It describes the internal hang-ups and neuroses that lie in the dark recesses of the psyche. It encompasses anything that we intentionally do not acknowledge or are just oblivious to. It can even include ego's tricky rationalizations for our behaviors that are motivated by our shadow.

Judgement is a main part of shadow energy. We judge people all the time, so much that it is hard to recognize what we are doing. We may occasionally hear ourselves speak about people we do not even know, condemning or praising them. Our judgement, though, has nothing to do with them; it is a distortion in our own mind. It is a constructed mental image, when in fact every human is a multidimensional, living mystery. We may understand part of their character or never understand even the slightest aspect of them. We may judge out of our own limited perspective, and our judgements can be quite harsh. Judgement blocks love, empathy, and compassion. It arises out of delusion and ultimately out of ignorance.

Similarly, bias and prejudice can be shadow, especially when they are internalized. We spew out bias without consciousness, and the effect can be quite harmful. Without reservation or awareness, we make biased comments and opinions about others because of their gender, lifestyle, race, or religion. Implicit bias is unconscious prejudice, functioning in the dark regions of mind unless people are motivated to do deep self-reflection. It is shocking to realize that we are not free from subtle prejudice toward others even while consciously telling ourselves the story that we are evolved and politically correct. We often tell good stories about ourselves in opposition to others whom we have identified as racist, bigoted, sectarian, or xenophobic. This not only creates an unhealthy moral pride but also gives us a false belief that we have no bad traits to work on. If people desire to have a more enlightened, kind society, then honest self-reflection begins the journey through the haunted ground of shadow, which is the part of the psyche where the demons of prejudice and bias have been pushed away from awareness.

Such denial takes place because inconvenient truths about ourselves can create an internal dilemma. The part of us that wants to be good and evolved becomes very uncomfortable when we see in others what we despise in ourselves. We often project this less evolved, shadow energy on others, labeling them as "redneck," "white supremacists," or "conservatives." We become extremely radical or militant in order to be politically correct, but the inner demons are well-fed, healthy, and happy in the shadows of our psyche.

In Tibetan Buddhism one of the main practices is self-reflection: checking our intentions and especially examining whether we have ulterior motives. Everything we do is shaped and determined by our motivation and intentions. Jigme Lingpa said,

> It is all dependent on whether your motivation is wholesome or unwholesome. Good and bad are not determined by your outward performance.

Outward performance can be misleading and can be poisoned with the wrong motivation, even though it appears noble. For example, drug cartels in Latin America might gain popularity because they funnel money into local civic projects like schools and social programs. Yet, they do not do this out of altruistic motivations but to gain popular acceptance so they can survive and continue selling drugs. It is important that religious organizations or spiritual celebrities who do inspiring charity programs examine their motivations and make sure that they are genuinely helping rather than just subliminally encouraging the masses to perceive them as an image of a divine, utterly good, loving, and compassionate person. In an unexamined situation, shadow can be driving motivation.

If motivation is good, whatever noble actions we do, large or small, can be regarded as virtue. Continually examining our motivation in all activities is necessary to keep us honest with ourselves. For example, building a giant stupa or Buddha statute, which is typically considered a meritorious deed, will produce no blessing if our motivation is flawed. Motivation is flawed if you are seeking fame or respect from the project. If you are coming from a purely benevolent place, then many blessings are generated. But egoic motivation can overshadow the merit from any otherwise well-intended action.

One of the Tibetan Buddhist practices is mental journal writing. It is a form of inner dialog, in which you advise yourself. Great masters wrote poetry and verses partly to bring to light subversive egoic motivations, making conscious their inner demons and neuroses. The Dzogchen master Shabkarpa wrote the poem "At the Heart of the Lake" as a dialogue between his ego and his wisdom, written as a ballad. Wisdom tries to chastise ego, but ego argues back with witty answers, saying that all the spiritual practitioners who revere wisdom really only respect me—ego. Therefore, ego says that he has won the hearts of everyone, and wisdom is the loser. This incredible poem demonstrates the inner commitment needed to examine shadow, whether by an accomplished master or an average Joe. A legendary eleventh-century spiritual master from Tibet named Geshe Ben also epitomized this form of self-reflection. There are many anecdotes about him told like folk tales in Tibetan households. One tells that he was meditating in his hermitage while expecting a visit from his patrons. Even though he was an ascetic, he still depended on their generosity for food and clothes and to support his retreat. To prepare for their visit, he had cleaned his altar beautifully. But while waiting for their arrival, he realized that his motivation in cleaning was solely to impress them so that they would continue their support. With this recognition, he threw a handful of dust on his altar, returning it to its previous condition. On hearing about this, Padampa Sangye said, "By throwing that dust, Geshe Ben made the best offering in all of Tibet!" Bringing shadowy impulses to the light of awareness cuts their power. Releasing them with a radical commitment to be free opens the path to liberation.

Traditional beginning methods in Buddhism emphasize renouncing or avoiding negative emotions and focusing instead on cultivating goodness. The methods taught in Vajrayana, and Chöd in particular, may seem to contradict these principles. Some people might be shocked when they hear about transforming negative emotions and welcoming obstacles as a path to liberation. Many spiritual traditions are like the beginning methods of Buddhism and teach followers to suppress inner negativity and withdraw from worldly activities, which actually tend to incite inner demons. These are traditions based on a dualistic view of good and bad rather than the Vajrayana view of the interdependence of all things. Vajrayana Buddhism teaches a nondual view in which no human experiences, even inner demons and conflicting emotions, are intrinsically bad. Rather, they are beyond any duality. They are simply part of life, like anything else. Vajrayana invites us to directly face these internal forces with a nonjudging, nondual attitude and to work with them skillfully instead of avoiding or maneuvering around them. The nondual view is based on the great emptiness, the true nature, which is the most essential principle for this path of Chöd.

3

Emptiness

S piritual awakening is not simply an esoteric idea. It is talked about all the time in conversation and in books. People sometimes describe how it happened to them. Everyone from Buddhists to New Age proponents describe it as some kind of new reality in which they see things differently, with new vision. It would be naïve, though, to think that all spiritual awakenings are the same. Though the same term might be applied, the experiences can be quite different. Rather than a cerebral understanding, spiritual awakening in Buddhism means to have a very direct experience of the true nature of reality, which is called *shunyata*, or emptiness.

The whole outlook of Chöd is based on the wisdom of emptiness. Early in her life, Machig Labdrön was profoundly influenced by the Prajnaparamita sutras, the scriptures on emptiness attributed to the Buddha, propagated in India by Nagarjuna, and later revered in Tibet and China. Her teachings on Chöd arose from a deep understanding and realization of emptiness. Chöd rituals, chants, and music would be meaningless, like superficial play-acting, without the wisdom of emptiness as its basis. In order to develop an inner understanding, Chöd practitioners need to both study the sutras and philosophy and meditate on the essential meaning of emptiness. Together, study and practice open our minds and hearts to understanding ultimate truth.

The experience of emptiness can sometime happen spontaneously, triggered by a simple catalyst, or in the midst of practice. This is no different than a gradual experience of emptiness, except that it comes in a momentary flash rather than after study and practice. It can be accompanied by a profound feeling of complete liberation. We experience the true nature of reality and recognize that our notion of reality had been an illusion until that moment. Though it may be difficult to pinpoint which causes and conditions lead to an opening such as this, it generally takes years of striving and effort with completely pure aspiration. Then, the inner conditions crack open into liberating awakening. Like the foundation and frame of a beautiful building, the awakened state is host to the ritual details of Chöd, which become like the painting and decorations within the house.

WHAT IS EMPTINESS?

What is emptiness? It is the ultimate truth in Mahayana Buddhism. This can be misleading if we are not clear about it. To some people, the term *ultimate truth* implies a truth that is independent, above all other truths, like a God or a supernatural being or a thing that is separate from everything else. But this misses the point. Emptiness is not a "thing." It is not a truth that can be extricated from everything else. If we regard emptiness as an enduring philosophy common to all traditions or a single metaphysical truth shared by other world religions, we inadvertently make it a further veil to awakening.

Interpretations of spiritual opening are not shared but are unique to each religion. In the nineteenth century, knowledge of Eastern religions and philosophy began to permeate the spiritual consciousness of the West. This happened as an outcome of many social and political changes. In many Western countries, science and industry began to eclipse religion, resulting in the separation of church and state. Secular society, free of religious constraints began to flourish. At the same time, many people began to emigrate to other countries, and explorers began to penetrate remote regions of India and Tibet. There was tremendous cross-fertilization of faiths, cultures, and ideologies. People then became more informed about each other's creeds, and this gave rise to a new narrative that the heart of all religions was the same: the Tao, godhead, the absolute, emptiness, and so on. Not only are they not the same, but even within the same religion individuals may describe them differently.

Without truly understanding the subtle meaning of a spiritual tradition, its rich and unique profundity can be lost in translation. We should carefully and wholeheartedly learn what each tradition has to offer before lumping them together. In the West, when people attempt to interpret God as nondual and nontheistic, they risk offending traditionalists. Their motivation often has to do with unifying humanity together through an all-encompassing narrative, as well as believing that the transcendent, absolute truth of all religions is the same. On the contrary, the ways many people understand the absolute truth of their own religion are not only not the same as one another but are often in opposition. For many, God is an omnipresent being. The absolute truth in Buddhism has nothing in common with this view. Similarly, the Tao may sound like God or emptiness, but the way most Taoists interpret it is not like the God of Christianity or the notion of emptiness in Buddhism. It is its own thing. Even though the Tao is supposed to be inconceivable and ineffable, and the Taoists do not think of it as a being, it is still a "thing," an underlying principle. Such an interpretation of the Tao leaves no room for a marriage between the Tao and emptiness. Some might say that anything that is regarded as ineffable is emptiness because it is too big to be comprehended or too sacred to be labeled or named. But merely labeling an experience as "ineffable" also does not necessarily convey the true experience of emptiness.

Emptiness is the nature of the way things are, the nature of reality. Therefore, the *Heart Sutra*, which is one of the shorter and condensed Prajnaparamita sutras, has the famous line, "Form is emptiness; emptiness is form. Emptiness is no other than form; form is no other than emptiness." This line holds the key to its subtle meaning: that emptiness is the nature of everything but is not separate from everything else. The sutra, recited by many Buddhist sects around the world, goes on to deconstruct every dimension of ego's self-clinging.

There is nothing mystical about emptiness. It is a down-to-earth way of understanding the truth and nature of all things. In many languages, emptiness is a noun, which automatically implies it is a thing. Because it is a noun, the word itself can hinder an authentic understanding. To Mahayanists it is beloved and most sacred, but people can be shocked when they realize that emptiness is not a sacred entity that is apart from reality. It is part of all ordinary phenomena like napkins, forks, and spoons and the natural world of trees, clouds, hummingbirds, or bubbles in water. It is equally a part of bioluminescent fish lighting up the deep blue sea and dust on the carpet.

Sometimes people have the instinct to search for a powerful, omnipresent force that can save them. This is the ego game that juxtaposes the savior and the lost soul. Within this game, the notion of emptiness can be easily placed on a pedestal as something that will save us from ourselves, as though it were almost a god. This is a total miscomprehension of what it is. Such miscomprehension happens all the time. Wise thinkers and mystics throughout history have courageously delved into this realm of emptiness. Many have concluded that we human beings are lost because of a fundamental ignorance about the nature of reality. The remedy, which brings happiness, freedom, and enlightenment, is awakening to the nature of reality, to the way things are. This is why Shantideva said, "One would be liberated through seeing the truth." The truth that he refers to is emptiness.

Sometimes there is a suspicion in us about the perceived reality. We may feel there is something fishy about it. In general, though, we tend to go along with perceived reality, and it seems that no one has a problem with it. Its not like everyone is going around telling each other they are deluded. In the paradigm of this perceived reality, we are the center of the universe and everything revolves around us. All the good and bad are determined in relationship to the self. We might say something is good because it is good for the self or bad because it is dangerous to the self. We might say something is beautiful because the self is attracted to it or ugly because there is aversion to it. But suspicion begins to lurk, eventually leading us to inquiry and reflection, which bring us to the brink of new insight. Eventually a profound awakening happens. Usually, this suspicion leads us to become philosophical or inspires us to investigate the great works of sages such as Nagarjuna. But we may again get attached to the concepts about the true nature of reality. Mental constructs about something transcendental can be easily confused with the actual experience, like going to a restaurant and eating the menu rather than the food. Or, as another example, imagine that you are wearing a veil in front of your eyes. Everything you see is distorted by the veil. In trying to see clearly but misunderstanding the problem, you put on more veils. This happens with philosophy: even though its purpose is to see the nature of reality, it can be self-defeating.

The process of awakening to emptiness begins with negation, rather than forming profound, grand concepts about the nature of reality. This is not the modus operandi of our usual thinking mind. Whenever thinking mind tries to solve a problem or understand reality, it wants to learn information or at least develop new concepts. This tendency of mind is often the biggest obstacle to direct experience of transcendence, or absolute truth. The Buddha himself taught negation-based meditation, as did later masters. Negation is not about acquiring concepts but about removing obstructing ideas and opinions of reality. In the beginning, it may seem that we are taking apart reality, but this is not what is happening. Rather, it is a deconstruction of the concepts about reality, not reality itself. Eventually we must let go of even negation itself. When the nature of reality is what it is, there is no need to add or take away anything from it. Resting in it is the perfect awakening.

This kind of negation is used in many systems, expressed by the well-known Sanskrit phrase *neti neti*, "not this, not that." It is a method of analytical meditation that helps wake us up to the true nature of things by first understanding what it is not. This method is also used in the Western tradition of apophatic theology, which asserts that human beings, because of their limitations, cannot comprehend God's essence or being. This is a striving to define God through understanding what he is not. Mysticism is based on the idea that the divine is not something that ordinary mind can understand. Similarly, such a method is used to understand the nature of reality by removing the conceptual veils and seeing what is there.

WHAT IS EMPTY OF WHAT?

A famous statement in the Mahayana tradition is "Pillar is empty of pillar." This may sound like it means that a pillar is not a pillar, but it is more than that. Why pillar? Because in the old days, every building had a pillar, both ordinary homes and temples. Everyone saw and lived with pillars everywhere. So, a pillar was an object of everyday life. This is similar to saying, in modern days, "Car is empty of car." This is powerful because if emptiness is defined by using an everyday object, it shakes our minds and has the power to open us to new insight. Seeing the ordinary and familiar as empty has the power to do this. If emptiness is described by saying something unusual, like "Horn of the dragon is empty of itself," it may not shake our minds. But if someone says, "Your smartphone is empty of smartphone," then it gets your attention and perhaps shakes your mind. You may look around, swivel in your chair toward that person, and say, "What do you mean?"

To say "Pillar is empty of pillar" is not to deny the pillar of being a pillar nor is it to deny the existence of a pillar. It is rather a rejection of a whole host of concepts and opinions that revolve around the pillar, including the more subtle ones where our perceiving minds simply take the pillar for granted. The purpose of this statement is to shake the mind into seeing things without the distortion of our concepts. It is meant to be unsettling and unreconcilable to our conceptual mind. What is being negated here is the notion of *svabhava*, or intrinsic nature. It is a tenet of Mahayana Buddhism that all things lack intrinsic nature. This view is considered the middle way between eternalism and nihilism.

Contrary to what some people have misunderstood, emptiness is far from nihilism, or the idea of nothingness. This is obvious because there *is* something here right now: we can see and hear and there is consciousness. But some people might have a misunderstanding of emptiness that has to do with a blank rejection of reality, like nihilism. Some might associate emptiness with rejecting sacredness or beauty. With the view of emptiness, we can continue to appreciate the world and all that we enjoy. It does not take anything away. Never worry that you are not able to enjoy life if you awaken to emptiness; it is rather the other way around. A whole source of suffering would go away because so much suffering arises from our own mind. Such awakening allows us to discover how beautiful life is. Our fears and greed no longer drown our consciousness in misery.

Emptiness is not a nihilistic point of view. It negates intrinsic nature but not anything else. For example, in our modern culture, our whole lives seem to be identified with our cell phones. We do not want to lose them for any reason and are attached to them like our own life blood. We are attached to the way they provide entertainment, how they hold all our contacts, give us access to the internet, and sustain our virtual connection with the world through endless social media. But cell phones, "smart" phones, have no intrinsic nature, or reality. Made of metal, glass, and plastic, they are not any one thing. And they cannot be separated from their components: they are inextricably, interdependently connected to the whole world. That is, without electricity, without humans who made electricity, without microchips and cellular technology, without the host of conditions that gave rise to cell phones being invented, we would not imbue them with any value. It is all the causes and interdependent conditions around them that have imbued cell phones with meaning. The extraordinary object that we are holding, with all its capability, is only labeled "cell phone." There is no cell-phoneness anywhere in this shiny shimmering object in our hand.

To understand this, we simply need to investigate, "Is it really a smartphone intrinsically?" No, it is not. Somehow the whole idea that this shiny object with colors and data and icons to push, that makes noise, songs, music, that we can use to talk to people, this thing that we call a smartphone is purely a mental construct that we superimpose on a collection of metal. It is not really a thing that has a separate, independent nature, which is that of being a smartphone.

SOCIETAL CONVENTIONS

Human beings are extremely intelligent, and consciousness is designed to be enlightened. So through simple inquiry, this turns out to be quite an easy matter to figure out. It does not take years and years to figure out what emptiness is. However, there are stories of students taking years in deep retreat, periodically meeting with grouchy Zen teachers who give them a koan, a provocative and unanswerable question to contemplate for years. When the student returns, the master still will not give his seal of approval because ultimate realization still has not occurred. These stories make us feel that emptiness is too profound to understand, but it is actually quite easy in some sense. And on the other hand, it is not easy either or else everyone would be awakened right now. It is more that there is resistance in our minds to waking up, rather than that the issue is too difficult or complicated. A simple way to think about emptiness and get around this resistance to understanding it is to think about the societal conventions we operate with that are easy to realize have no fixed reality. For example, borders between countries have no intrinsic reality. On one side of the line people say, "This is the United States," and on the other, "This is Mexico (or Canada)." But borders have been changing all the time. The United States was much smaller until lands were taken from Mexicans, Hawaiians, and Native Americans. A border is just a piece of land. It has no intrinsic reality.

Astronaut Scott Kelly looked back at the earth from two hundred and fifty miles into space and said, "You see continents and countries without any political borders. It gives you the impression that we are all in this thing called humanity together. Actually, the whole experience makes you feel insignificant." His vantage point and perception offered a rare perspective on the precious, unbounded planet we live on. Before countries were settled and defined, the land was just the land; the construct of countries did not exist. Before the First World War, Germany was the Austro-Hungarian empire, which does not exist anymore. The British empire, on which it used to be said "the sun never sets," has morphed and changed over time, sometimes expanding, sometimes losing ground. Now it is a little country, a little island. Borders are arbitrary, and the idea of a country is arbitrary.

In the same way, race is also arbitrary. Pinpointing where one race ends and another begins, even using genotyping, is hard to determine. Can we absolutely determine where white people started? Was it in Morocco, Sweden, or Germany? When you look, it is hard to find one perfect line. We cannot distinguish an absolute line from which everyone from here to there is Middle Eastern or European.

Human history came from one source, and everyone started traveling. There is no single gene for whiteness, no primordial race, no Asian-ness or Indian-ness. These distinctions never really existed. We created racial distinction for certain reasons. The distinctions serve some purposes but are pointless if you believe they have intrinsic truth. This view causes all sorts of problems, such as war and genocide. Humans can be very destructive when we believe in our mental constructs. The point is not to reject all these divisions but to realize that they lack intrinsic reality. It is not that suddenly everyone must deny their race, nationality, or ethnicity. It is more that we can see that the identities are resting on rickety ground, supported by mental constructs and beliefs. While many are attached to these divisions, there is also a deep longing in humanity to transcend them. Such sentiment is quite strong, which may be why John Lennon's song "Imagine" has been so popular around the world and is played at major events, including the Olympics. The song tells us that it is easy to imagine that there are no countries and nothing that should justify killing or dying. By eliminating the concept of "boundary," the conceptual territories of possessiveness, self-identification, and enemies are also eliminated.

We can also easily see the emptiness of societal conventions in beauty and wealth. Society admires outer physical beauty, which is an illusion. Through the "neti" approach, the illusion of outer beauty can be deconstructed: beauty turns out to be subjective, and if we question the notion of beauty, we cannot find beauty in the object itself. It comes down to one's own perception. This fact opens up the possibility for us to reevaluate the experience of beauty. It gives us the opportunity to begin to appreciate inner beauty and put value on it. Similarly, the emptiness of wealth and power is revealed when we inquire into the very notion. The wealthy, powerful person was not born rich or powerful. Their whole identity is something society superimposed on them at some point in their life. If that person loses money, the idea of being rich is already transient. Where is the line that makes someone wealthy? Which dollar made them hit the wealthy mark? Furthermore, even the rich can not be denied their humanity, as everyone is vulnerable deep down. No matter what image or mask of invincibility they project on to the world, there are always challenges that can take away the mask and reveal their vulnerability.

Longchenpa describes in his writings how enslaved we can be from buying into the conventions of the world. He teaches how to be free from them in these lines:

Let go of the fear of not pleasing others, conventionality,
and sycophancy.

Do not gather wealth out of fear of being poor.
Let go of planning due to fear of future woes.
Do not strive for prestigious positions out of fear of
  inferiority.
Let go of worldly values due to fears of being flawed.
Do not upset others by believing in your superiority.

In this verse Longchenpa perfectly describes that buying into conventions causes us to suffer from feeling insignificant and gives us a general sense of inadequacy, an inferiority complex that springs from believing we are not as good, intelligent, attractive, or important as others. We do really weird things to try to compensate for these holes in our consciousness, losing dignity and becoming like sheep without the courage to forge our own path. We end up not knowing who we really are or what we really want. These lead us to do unbenevolent actions, like pleasing one person by putting someone else down. The collective human value system, in itself, has no intrinsic reality.

The underlying layer of this superficial mindset is a strong desire to be authentic and not sell out our principles. But there is also a strong desire for the seemingly tempting reward for playing the games of the modern world. The desire for authenticity intentionally shuts itself down to avoid inner conflict. We can be in turmoil with two strong forces pulling us in different directions. Without being able to admit it, we vicariously fulfill the desire for authenticity through admiration for enlightened icons, mystics, rebels, renunciates, and iconoclasts. We all admire them but very few have the willingness to do what it takes to be like them. Conventional value systems have a grip on our consciousness and are so convincing that it is difficult to resist them. We can be enslaved by conventions, and it is truly difficult to be free inside when you are part of human society.

Understanding emptiness unveils the illusion of misperceiving reality. In this context, illusion means that our thoughts and beliefs rule what we think and believe, rather than truly perceiving what is. It is not some sort of innocuous, harmless illusion, but instead it has a powerful destructive impact on us. Many of our conventional value systems and worldviews are simply built upon this illusion. These illusions cause suffering in us until their falsehood is clearly seen.

In Tantric Buddhism there are wrathful deities called *heruka*, or "blood drinkers," who embody indivisible bliss and emptiness. Their form is wrathful, often holding a skull cup of blood, brandishing a butcher's knife, or pointing a *purbha*, a sacred dagger. They trample on or drive a stake through the heart of illusion that is represented by various demon beings. This whole morbid image is a powerful demonstration that enlightenment mercilessly, radically dismantles illusion. Vajrakilaya is an example of a heruka who has many forms and is perhaps the most revered heruka in the Nyingma tradition. His expression is often wrathful, as his wisdom destroys the army of negative forces and illusion seen as demons.

Emptiness can be benevolent, but often its energy can be experienced as challenging to ego. It can appear to be wrathful because it dismantles illusions. Dismantling is only challenging because ego resists letting go and does not have the wisdom to know what is good for us. We often hold on to these illusions because they are familiar to us and they have been the sole version of our reality. They give us a false sense of certainty and security. And yet, being under the power of illusion is full of suffering. Our ego does not want to let go of illusion since it is like jumping off the ledge of a high building. Ego wants to stay on the ledge no matter how sorrowful or treacherous it can be. Awakening frightens ego to go away from the edge of the known and go to the edge of the unknown.

Periodically, just by some kind of benevolence of the universe or by the blessings of our own buddha nature, a crack opens in our consciousness that naturally allows us to tap into emptiness. Such opening can sometimes be unsettling or liberating, depending on whether we are ready to embrace what the universe is showing us. If there is any kind of resistance, the opening can turn into a crisis, because what happens is that your whole paradigm of reality is shaken. Sometimes there is nothing you can hold on to. You feel that any concept of reality, or sense of the known, falls into pieces and no longer works as it did. This can literally cause an existential crisis. There are stories of Buddhist monks who were scared when they first heard the teachings on emptiness for this reason. Existential crises are not fun experiences to have. But once the opening has happened, it is hard to go back to the old paradigm of reality. On the other hand, if there is no resistance, the opening can be very liberating. The very root of our suffering is challenged. Suffering exists in the paradigm of illusion. Outside of that, there is pure freedom.

Another reason we resist emptiness is that we think that if we lose the sense of intrinsic nature, then life will be just one big thing that has no subtleties and no diversity and we would be lost in holy boredom and would not have any rich feelings like admiration, love, will, intention, desire, or passion. This is not true. We can live a colorful life, still laugh and cry and love, even if intrinsic nature is transcended. We may begin to enjoy life even more—it could be playful. We may be able to stop taking everything so seriously. The joyous spirit within will awaken. Perhaps we would not take life so seriously. It could be carefree, spacious, enjoyable play.

Awakening to emptiness can happen spontaneously and can also be cultivated. Though spontaneous glimpses of transcendence occur without meditating, traditional Buddhist practices help us to have a direct experience of emptiness and be able to live this experience. In this way, the experience becomes part of your life. One method is inquiry, which is exemplified in the Buddhist school of thought known as Madhyamaka. This is a profound, nitty-gritty method of inquiry into the nature of everything. By closely examining and inquiring into things, we eventually pierce the veil of intrinsic nature, thus finding emptiness. Techniques of inquiry, such as Madhyamaka, powerfully work to help us experience emptiness, especially when our consciousness become deluded. The technique can help pierce delusion because nothing other than the consciousness itself is creating the delusion. There is no one outside who is making consciousness deluded. The source of delusion is *avidya*, unawareness. This is the part of the state of consciousness itself that is lacking in insight into the nature of reality and then gives space for the consciousness to become deluded. Once consciousness becomes deluded, it continues to get caught up in concepts, ideas, and misperceptions, which are its own display. That web of delusion can continue forever. Yet, somehow, consciousness also feels the impulse to wake up from delusion. Once that happens, we can engage with inquiries and investigations as a whole effort to untie the traps of illusion that bind consciousness itself.

Machig Labdrön said, "In Buddhism, notions of dharmakaya and buddhahood are considered the most sacred, yet in inquiry these should not be exempt from contemplations into emptiness. They should be brought into the light of inquiry because they also lack intrinsic nature." Thus, even the most desirable achievement of Buddhism, the final object of all Buddhist practice is negated. She is transcending the intrinsic nature of buddhahood but clearly not rejecting the state of awakening. She is only rejecting clinging and identification with buddhahood, the subtle holding on to it as a way of self-grasping.

Metaphorically speaking, emptiness is like a brilliant sun that illuminates the whole world, and we are resisting its brilliance. We are like those who have been living in a dark dungeon and are at first blinded by the brilliance when they see the sun. Or we are like someone who has never eaten fruit, and when they first do, the taste is so intense, so delicious, that it is difficult to tolerate. Emptiness invites us to total freedom. If we hold on to anything, we are not liberated one hundred percent. Such radical transcendence of duality prevails and is central to the Prajnaparamita sutras. Some say the line that caused Machig Labdrön's awakening to emptiness, was the instruction that if we are attached to anything—from form all the way to the buddha mind—the attachment should be regarded as the work of *mara*, the archetypal demon whose sole vocation is to cause hinderances on our path to enlightenment. So, we should not get attached to anything, including the buddha mind.

This is the most difficult thing to understand. When someone embodies the wisdom of emptiness, completely free from all worldly bondages, they may reside in the human world but not be troubled by conventions. Fear and greed become passing, transitory states and occur within unshakable equanimity. The usual chains of conditioned existence do not torture them.

Tibetans traditionally consider that one aspect of an enlightened person is that they can get angry but not fixate on it. The enlightened person does not hold on to anger but has the ability to let go of it and does not elaborate or reinforce it. To enter the path of emptiness—of making friends with it and understanding it—is to aspire for such awakening and eventually live all the time in this nondual view, or reality. This path requires diligence and honesty in investigating the nature of reality, not clinging to anything no matter how much we cherish it but seeing it as being of the same empty nature as everything. We can see that good, bad, happy, and sad are all in the nature of reality. Therefore, without bias toward one state or the other, we fall in love with the world.

4

Ritual and Liturgy

My aim in writing this book is to demystify certain Buddhist rituals, so that they are not clumped together with shamanism and so that their implications for everyday life can be better understood. Many people see all Buddhist rituals as being the same, so I hope to clarify the underlying meaning of the rituals in Chöd and distinguish them from others. Though there is symbolic meaning in some aspects of the practices, such as the use of a bone trumpet, clothing, special drums, liturgical songs, and all the paraphernalia, Chöd has a practical effect on our lives. Some might mistakenly consider Chöd a shamanic practice or view it as an eccentric form of spiritual entertainment, but this would be misleading.

Human beings have used rituals since the dawn of civilization as a way to magically communicate with the supernatural world. Using ritual is often an effort to manipulate the seen and unseen forces of the natural world so that it fits the desires of people.

Rituals often include chanting, incantations, and the use of ceremonial implements. However, the rituals in Buddhism are not considered magic. They are not about using supernatural powers to control natural or spiritual forces. Rather, they are for the purpose of changing your consciousness. This is the big difference between spiritual disciplines like Buddhism and ancient shamanic practices. Buddhist rituals are not only spiritual but also cultural and can serve as a medium for transforming our consciousness by offering practical techniques to train the mind. Unless someone has this understanding of Buddhist rituals, some of them can be misunderstood as shamanic practices.

Many people have misused Chöd by disconnecting it from its original teachings and turning it into a magical endeavor. But even as early as the twelfth century, the Dzogchen master Patrul Rinpoche warned against this. He warned people not to practice Chöd as hocus-pocus or simply to garner donations from patrons who hired them to help with sickness or bad circumstances. Some Chöd practitioners in those days would make quite a performance out of the ritual practice, turning it into ancient performance art by rolling their eyes and using weird body language. In this way, they hoped to receive more donations from their patrons. Somehow, the grander the performance, the more effective some naïve patrons felt the ritual would be. Patrul Rinpoche wrote a satirical poem pointing out that such practitioners were misusing Chöd to prey on the gullibility of others and gather donations, but in the end what they were doing was not true Chöd.

As a Buddhist teacher, I have been introducing elaborate Buddhist rituals in the West for many years. Unlike shamanic ceremonies, these rituals are based on working with our minds and not on controlling the world around us. I witness powerful, transformative effects on the people who practice them and aspire to continue introducing Chöd to students as long as they are interested. Why use elaborate melodies, instruments, and ritual when it seems that we could cut through self-grasping on the spot without them? It is possible to cut through on the spot, but using ritual as a structure helps bring wandering mind back into the present moment of practice. When we are overwhelmed by emotions and inner conflict, external forms can provide a neutral ground to come back to. They also help intensify aspiration, visualization, and the whole experience.

If someone knows the significance of a particular ritual and correctly applies it to experience inner awakening, it becomes a powerful catalyst. This is why there are rituals in all sects within Buddhism. Some of them are practiced in every tradition, but some are unique to each one—Zen, Theravada, Vajrayana, and so on. For example, there is a monastic practice that is observed in many Buddhist traditions, called *sojong* in Tibetan. In this, monks and nuns come together for bimonthly confession to restore their broken precepts. In general, the monastics are required to practice a very specific set of observances, such as specific behaviors regarding dressing, eating, chanting, and meditating. These are all laid out in the monastic code, called the *vinaya*. Ordained practitioners take precepts relating to wearing robes, shaving the head, and fasting after noon. All these rituals and observances help to remind them of their vows and invite the world to witness their commitment to spiritual discipline.

Another example of a traditional ritual held in many Buddhist monasteries is the monsoon retreat. Its origin goes back to the time of the Buddha. Guidelines for the retreat are quite strict and orderly, including restricting monks from leaving the retreat area until the retreat ends. How strictly the retreats are held depends on the monastery. When I was a monk, I attended a few monsoon retreats in the Nyingma lineage. Our abbot implemented traditional strict guidelines. Everyone had to get up early every morning. Two monks would blow the conch three times: first as a wake-up call, second to get ready, and third to come to the temple. Many of the younger monks did not like the sound of the conch blowing; it was not pleasant to their ears. In front of the temple, someone would beat the *gandi*, a rhythm instrument. Everyone had to rinse their mouths with water poured into their hands from a pitcher. Once they entered the temple, they would sit and the abbot would lead the session. The ceremony, beginning with chanting and prostrations, could go on for the whole day with a long lunch break. Part of the ritual was to observe fasting from after lunch until the next morning. There were liturgies to chant before and after eating. Now and then some lay people would come and sponsor our lunch, and at that time everybody would come to the temple to eat in silence. Everyone ate slowly and mindfully, following the ritual guidelines.

In the beginning, I had strong resistance to these strict rules. I was young and wanted to be physically active. But after a week, I began to enjoy the retreat and was sad when it ended. The rituals turned out to be conducive for us to cultivate conscientiousness, carefulness, and dignity. Chöd, too, has its own ritual and observances that can help someone succeed in their practice, but they are quite different from the vinaya system. Chöd is a radical path because it is all about letting go of hope and fear and cutting away conventional traps.

MOTIVATION

Before learning the specific rituals of Chöd, we need to set the right motivation for engaging in the practice. We have to ask ourselves, "Why am I doing Chöd in the first place?" Genuine motivation is the wish to cut through self-grasping and drop the chain of duality, hope, and fear. It is the wish to be completely free and to develop boundless compassion and love, which radiates to all beings. It is the intention to be truly honest with ourselves, to see our own inner poisons, to be willing to cut identification with them, and to help others wake up to their own innate wisdom. When we aspire to practice Chöd, it is important to look inward and make the vow, "May I enter this path, reveal inner demons, cut identification with them, and develop love and compassion for the benefit of others."

Without awareness, ego's tricks can easily slip past us, even when we are sincerely committed to working with them. As we sharpen our awareness, we quickly begin to see and face the undertow of ulterior motivations. Those forces cause us to act and behave from ego's ambition. The whole practice can then become another holy compulsion that will not change our consciousness in the true sense. I have discussed this with other lamas, and we all feel concerned about it. In the East, many people practice Chöd with all the paraphernalia—long hair, *damaru* drum, trumpet, and charming melodies—but we wonder how many of them know what they are really doing.

Our more hidden motivations are often the most difficult to acknowledge, and we are often trapped by them. Though we may superficially acknowledge them, they are frequently rationalized, and their darker sides may stay hidden in ego's contrivances. A central principle of Buddhism emphasizes continually checking our motivation, becoming aware of ego's input into them. Right motivation includes replacing ulterior motives with authentic altruism, love, and compassion. It is the intention to wake up and dedicate ourselves to the benefit of others.

For example, during the lockdown of COVID 19 in 2020, I had lots of time to stay at home and do things I did not have time for before. I started writing and speaking to many people virtually, including a Chödpa named Anam Lama Komdra, who is in his seventies. People told me he was a serious Chödpa who still observed the traditional way of practicing Chöd. I became quite interested in speaking to him. The person who connected us mentioned that Lama Komdra had recently gone to Lhasa on pilgrimage. It was the first time that he had let anyone take a picture of him. While the picture was being taken, he made a prayer, "Whoever sees this picture, may they find joy." This may sound weird to Westerners, but it is truly inspiring and sincere, as simple as a child's wish. He normally did not want pictures taken of himself, because he did not want to foster vanity. But he made this exception as an expression of his altruism and wish to create goodness in the world.

I was told that Lama Komdra typically lived a humble life, accepting few donations, and I wanted to learn more from him. I thought we would just have a simple chat. But this is not how it worked, as he lives in a different state of consciousness. He asked me to recite some prayers, and I asked him the same. He then started to speak spontaneously: "May we be able to embrace everyone and anyone, regardless of who they are, not judging whether they are attractive or not, wealthy or not, and that we be able to have compassion and love for all." He kept going for a while. I was moved because he was not just reciting a traditional prayer, but these sincere wishes came from the bottom of his heart without pretense. He is a true seer. He is a living example of how traditional Chöd practices and structures, with pure motivation, can transform and take someone's consciousness to a higher place. After our conversation, his words continued to resonate with me. I felt that our conversation was profound advice that I should remember the rest of my life if I can.

EMPOWERMENT

In general, empowerment is tantric initiation through which someone vows to hold samaya, the tantric precept, and becomes a *tantrika*. Often the empowerment is associated with a particular mandala or deity and gives someone permission to practice a particular sadhana. Its true purpose is to let the recipient experience the nature of mind. Anybody who wants to do traditional Chöd practice must first do ngöndro, which is the preliminary practice in the Vajrayana tradition. *Ngöndro* literally means "that which goes before." Traditionally ngöndro has certain essential components covering a wide range of spiritual practices that allow the individual to experience the whole spectrum of spiritual consciousness, including love, compassion, and purification.

In the context of Chöd, we make the commitment to sever attachment to conflicting emotions. An elaborate traditional empowerment ceremony, called *abhisheka*, is performed once someone has completed ngöndro. An abhisheka is a Vajrayana ritual meant to awaken wisdom in the mind of the disciple. In receiving it, we are empowered to follow a particular spiritual practice. A person who wants to practice Chöd requests three things from a guru, or lama: reading transmission, abhisheka, and instructions. During the reading transmission the guru reads the liturgy out loud and through this confers upon the practitioner the lineage blessings and permission to practice a specific Chöd liturgy. Empowerment is a much more elaborate ceremony than this, after which the guru gives extensive teachings on Chöd. All the ceremonies and fanfare instill a strong feeling that you are really committed to this path.

During the abhisheka we take samaya, a sacred commitment to the path of Chöd. Samaya is a precept in the Vajrayana, or tantra tradition. The list of the samayas is different in each tantric system, but in general there are fourteen. "Sacred commitment" may sound like serious business. The idea is that we should try to follow them as much as possible, but the tradition expects that we may breach them. They can then be restored through a special ritual called *ganachakra*. Some say that the major difference between monastic precepts and the samaya is that the monastic vows are like breaking a clay vessel, which cannot be repaired, whereas breaking a tantric samaya is like damaging a copper vessel, which can be fixed. When the primary monastic vows are broken, it means that one is no longer a monastic; the vows cannot be repaired. However, even if the primary tantric precepts are broken, the practitioner can do ceremonies to repair the broken precepts and continue to be a tantrika.

INSTRUMENTS AND IMPLEMENTS

Many of the traditional Chödpas are free of material possessions, with few exceptions. They carry only a one-pole tent to sleep in during their journeys to the haunted ground and little else. The simple tent symbolizes their inner and outer journeys. Some Chödpas travel for days and days, camping at different sites.

Each of the ritual implements used in Chöd practice have an allegorical meaning. There are variations of the practice that use any combination of these implements. The *kartika* is a small, hand-held ritual knife, known as the knife of the dakinis. It symbolizes cutting through attachment to conventional value systems through ultimate insight into emptiness. There is a trumpet made of bone, which symbolizes bringing all devas and demons under our power. The drum is known as a damaru, which symbolizes trampling on duality and awakening to nonduality. The ritual bell, known as a *ghanta*, symbolizes magnetizing *dakas* and dakinis, who are male and female deities with the spiritual power to go everywhere through space. By attracting them, they become our allies on the path. The skull cup, or *kapala*, is related to detachment and transformation of the world we experience and is a reminder of our impermanence.

Some Chödpas use a skull cup in everyday life, and for them it is more than just ritual paraphernalia. They use it as a bowl or cup to eat and drink from, often not using ordinary containers at all. It is no longer common to find these Chödpas, but those who use the skull cup in everyday life do it because it has a specific meaning. Though some may find its use for eating and drinking as repulsive and barbaric, for Chödpas it is a reminder of the impermanent nature of human life. It helps cut through attachment to worldly glory, self-indulgence, and hedonism, and it frees us from concepts of beauty and attraction.

Chöd is like a counterculture Dharma. The instruments and implements symbolize the free spirit of Chöd practice and a way of life that is simple and carefree. A follower of this path is not part of a big organization but is on their own, not going along with the conventions of big institutions. Chödpas have a sense of individualism, not in the egoic sense but as those who dedicate their lives to this practice, to living and practicing alone, unlike their monastic brethren. Practicing within an institution, with rules and regulations and a strict code of conduct, makes it hard to conduct the carefree practice of a yogi.

OBSERVANCES

Ritual is the outward performance of ceremony, singing, chanting, or dancing. Observance is adhering to the outward disciplines, such as fasting and abstinence. Observances vary from one tradition to another. There are both rituals that are baked into the practice tradition and simple, practical instructions. Especially when we do retreat in the haunted ground, we observe the four feasts of Chöd and also follow simple guidelines like not shouting at night and not walking with bare feet.

Observances that we follow during a Chöd retreat—such as not combing our hair, shaving, or taking a bath—help us let go of all vanity. We let ourselves be completely natural, not getting lost in taking care of our physical image or squandering precious time fixing it. When we fix our image, not only does it take time but it is commonly an exercise in ego—wanting to be presentable and charming or elicit admiration from others. During intensive retreats, it is most effective to abandon the focus on self-care and grooming. Following prescribed observances can, like anything, become a holdout of ego. In following Chöd observances, the Chödpa is continually cutting the tendency to fixate on them.

Chödpas are outside of society in many ways, but at the same time they are very much within it. Other cultures are on to this as well. For example, the Lakota people of the Great Plains of North America often have a special tribal member called *heyoka*, a contrarian who does everything opposite to the norm. They are not crazy but are regarded as sacred clowns who serve the tribe by saying things others are afraid to say, acting as a mirror to the tribe's fears, wearing their clothes backward, riding backward on a horse, and acting outrageously. They wake people up from taking themselves too seriously and show how to break free of their confinements. The heyoka holds a ceremonial role and helps members stay in healthy relationship to themselves, each other, and the ever-changing world.

Most social conventions are developed to keep relation with the world around us from being overwhelming. Though we go along with them, people often have a secret desire to let their hair down. But anything can be turned into a constraining convention. Even leading a lifestyle that is unconventional can become a convention itself. This is something that people must pay attention to. While we try to go beyond ego, it can easily outsmart us. Someday, we wake up and realize we have been completely fooled by ego, all the while believing we were getting somewhere. The master Jigme Lingpa in fact did not follow many of the observances we might expect. He is an example of a master who let go of any identification. Even though he was a renunciate and celibate, he did not wear monastic robes, like the orange shawl, and did not shave his head. Human ego can take on anything and turn it into something else. Even the purest spiritual practices can turn into something that serves ego's purposes.

ROBES AND CLOTHING

For Western Buddhist monastics, wearing a robe can be trickier than in the East where robes are part of the culture. Here in the West, a robe-clad person is seen as exotic. But when we go into the wilderness, there is no public to impress. In the end the robe does not matter. You can wear any clothes when you practice Chöd.

In Buddhism there are two main robes: the tantrika's robe and the monastic robes. Monastic robes are often red or yellow. The tantrika's are white. Chödpas also wear specific robes that are unique to this practice. The clothing of Chöd is called the fashion of a *herukapa*, or cemetery fashion. In Vajrayana Buddhism, herukas are a category of wrathful deities who are enlightened beings. They often adopt a fierce countenance, which symbolizes the ethos of an unconventional, carefree yogic lifestyle.

The musical instruments and robes of the Chödpa are known as the fashion of the *kusal*, meaning "yogi" or "spiritual vagabond." *Kusali* describes someone who walks the path of a Chödpa, who has renounced ordinary life. Their clothing is the fashion of the charnel ground: a simple white shawl called a *zankar*. These are also worn on occasion by other practitioners. Some Tibetan Buddhist paintings show lineage holders, such as Milarepa, in relaxed posture and wearing the same kind of white shawl. In the context of Vajrayana this shawl signifies the natural state: uncontrived, carefree, the nature of mind, or buddha mind. In Chöd it also symbolizes the path of Chöd itself, which cuts through all worldly concerns and concepts, the path that turns our worldview upside down.

When I first came to the United States, I lived in the mountains of Santa Cruz, California. On occasions when I would go downtown, I would see people with dreadlocks playing didgeridoos. Their clothes were plain, none carried designer accessories, like Gucci purses, and they did not cut their hair. They had a very natural look, and I thought, "These could be regarded as some kind of Western Chödpas." This led me to believe there is a universality in this style of fashion, which is used to express the counterculture ethos and the carefree and unconventional spiritual pursuit.

The culture within monasteries is also quite distinct. Along with beautiful discipline and complete commitment to practice, people spend lots of time fixing their image, making sure they are clean and have perfectly shaved heads. If they are a yogi, they comb their hair beautifully. People commit many hours and much effort to their robes, folding them beautifully, precisely washing them, ironing them to perfection, and attending to how they are draped and worn. This is just like people paying attention to secular fashions. In Seoul, South Korea, I have seen specialty stores that stock very pricey monks' and nuns' robes. There can be a lot of materialism around monastic clothing and appearance, and in this way it is no different from what we encounter in all sectors of society. This is not to say that this is necessarily a hinderance to their enlightenment— not at all. It can be uplifting to tend to our clothes, to pay attention and bring dignity. But it is also good to have time in life to be free from the chains of any conventions in our mind. They dominate us in everyday life. I often encourage people to enter a period in their lives where they completely drop all conventions.

Robes, like uniforms, have power. Once, while traveling from Los Angeles to the San Francisco Bay Area, I stopped by a bizarre and wild hotel called Madonna Inn. As I passed the bar, I saw a fellow in blue jeans wearing a Tibetan monk's jacket, drinking and smoking. He seemed to think his outfit was cool and exotic. People like robes because they inspire obedience and reverence in others. Fourteen or fifteen years ago, I taught a weekend retreat in Mexico, not too far from the city of Guadalajara. While I was there, I wore a *shamtab*, which is a kind of monastic robe that looks like a skirt. At a restaurant, I asked the waitress for the bill, and she said, "It's on the house." Having not yet learned this idiom, I did not understand what she meant and then realized that she was giving it to me for free. Seeing my traditional red skirt, the waitress identified me as a representative of a holy tradition. Even though it was not her own, she generously honored my tradition by giving me this meal. I was touched. On top of the huge heart and generosity of Mexican culture, she saw me as a spiritual person because of my clothing.

I stopped wearing robes eleven or twelve years ago. In examining my own motivations, it felt funny to wear robes when I was no longer a monk, and it was a huge psychological change for me to let go of the traditional clothes. The change did not happen overnight. The part of me that identified with the role of monk and the non-monastic part went back and forth in inner dialogue. Like others who follow traditions and wear monastic garb, I had deep identification with the robes I wore. Giving them up was an opportunity to question my motivation and my identification and also reflect on how others viewed me. I had to ask myself, "Will I still be regarded as a spiritual teacher, if I teach in khaki pants?"

The purpose of wearing robes is not to elicit reverence, to impress others, or to have some invisible authority but to remind us of our motivations in spiritual practice. I found that after letting go of wearing robes, my motivation to practice and teach was the same, because the robes were only an outward sign of an inward practice that had never diminished in me. Chödpas in Tibet who dedicate their lives to Chöd practice live carefree all the time. They are almost like volunteers who remind people to be careful and not be totally trapped by all the rules and trends and styles and fashion and etiquette. These are man-made and have no intrinsic value. If we take them too seriously, they bind us and cause an enormous amount of suffering. So now and then there are these awakened individuals who live a life of unconventionality and point to transcendence beyond the world, who are utterly free. As a lifelong path, it is arduous, but many cultures have these unusual, wise individuals who do things unconventionally in order to wake themselves and others up.

LITURGY AND MELODY

Ancient, rich, and profound Chöd liturgies and teachings have been handed down for centuries in spiritual lineages of Tibetan Buddhism. Composed by great masters of those traditions— such as Longchenpa, Tsongkhapa, Karma Chagme, Dharmashri, Rangjung Dorje, and many more—they have been handed down through a succession of teachers and disciples and are studied and practiced even today. Individuals may choose to practice a given liturgy because of their lineage or because their guru recommended it for them.

Whether a short or long liturgy, and with varying central figures, the source of all Mahamudra Chöd practices are attributable to Machig Labdrön, the founder of the Chöd tradition in Tibet. It is common to find Machig Labdrön herself as the central figure in many Chöd liturgies. Other liturgies have as the principal figure Yum Chenmo, the great mother, who represents the embodiment of transcendent wisdom. Nyingmapas consider Machig Labdrön to be an emanation of Yeshe Tsogyal, and all consider her to be an emanation of Yum Chenmo. In this iconography Yum Chenmo is golden in color with two arms. All the buddhas and enlightened beings are born through awakening to the wisdom of emptiness, so the symbology is a mother who gives birth to this awakening. In Jigme Lingpa's Chöd liturgy, *The Dakini's Laughter*, the main figure in the guru yoga section is Padmasambhava. He is surrounded by the assembly of dakas and dakinis, representing the radiant display of awakened mind.

The traditional structures of Chöd liturgies have slightly different stages depending on their origin, but most, including *The Dakini's Laughter*, contain the vajra dance, refuge, bodhicitta, mandala offering, guru yoga, and then the four feasts—white, variegated, red, and black.

The Chöd melodies are distinct from other Buddhist chants. They have their own musical and liturgical niche. Each Chöd liturgy has its own specific music for the bell, damaru, bone trumpet, and liturgical song. The melody is meant to invoke specific experiences in the practitioners. Melodies change throughout the liturgy, expressing the meaning within each section. Some sound like folk music, and others are like a haunting expression of deep yearning for awakening. Chöd melodies are often regarded as sacred in themselves, because they are attributed to a great master. Some say that the Buddhist master Jigme Lingpa developed *The Dakini's Laughter* melodies after seeing a vulture's flight. But the truth is that even within Tibet, people sing these melodies differently. It is possible that the melodies change depending on the places they are sung and the musical key that each chanter uses.

There are two ways of singing Chöd, the monastic and the folk style. The monastic style, though varying from one monastery to another, tends to use very low registers, within fewer octaves. The folk style uses higher ranges and sometimes more octaves. Musical flow in the folk-song style is very uplifting, helping to inspire and arouse the aspiration of the liturgy. For many people the deeper tones are more meditative and powerful and are easier to sing in unison with everyone's voices blending together. The folk songs, with their higher registers, are possibly how a lone yogi in the mountains may choose to sing. Some suspect that as wandering Chödpas traveled around, they sang higher and louder in order to attract and entertain people. Both forms require training and dedication. Once people get used to it, the music and liturgy have a strong impact on our experience during practice.

Melody and ritual are not essential to Chöd practice. They can also become yet another "fashion," something the practitioner takes pride in or clings to, preventing them from relaxing into the natural state the way they might be able to more easily without all the music and instruments. Someone can perfect the form but have no real understanding of the meaning within the practice. If approached this way, these practices will have no liberating effect. One of my aspirations as a Buddhist teacher is to let people from different walks of life taste the liberating effects of Chöd, without requiring them to do all the rituals. During meditation retreats, I have invited people to practice Chöd without liturgy, music, or instruments in order to work with their inner demons and, in silence, let go of identification with them. People have told me that this way of practicing Chöd has been very effective.

As I mentioned earlier, many people in Asia currently practice Chöd. Their gatherings can almost seem like Chöd conventions. People come together with damarus and bells, all of which are mass manufactured. They all expertly play the melodies and music, but sometimes I wonder how many have the right motivation behind the performance. It is very easy to miss the point with Chöd, just as with other practices. Machig Labdrön warned that there would be both misunderstanding and misuse of this technique. She left warnings and advice so that her tradition would not be misunderstood in the future. Some of her advice was based on the fact that authentic Chöd needs to be supported by clear motivation and the wisdom of nonduality.

In the old days, Tibetans used Chöd as an exorcism to purify a haunted house or to cure people who were having a psychotic break. They were told that these negative conditions were caused by mischievous demons from outside. They practiced Chöd using their anger, rather than wisdom, to try to punish and subdue these external demons. But their misunderstanding lacked the wisdom of nonduality and the motivation of compassion. In today's world, we see the same abuse and misunderstanding of the practices. The wisdom of Chöd can be obscured by fixation on the ritual and the simple entertainment value of the music. A Chödpa must have a clear and strong motivation and aspiration to attain a profound understanding of emptiness and develop compassion.

5

Vajra Dance

In addition to the rich methods of visualization, yogic practices, and meditation, tantric Buddhism includes the important practice of vajra dance. This is a ritual element performed in the spirit of joyful confidence and triumph, either physically or energetically through visualizations. Many Tibetan Buddhist lineages include human enactments of deities dancing, dressed in costumes, and performing dances in the context of ritual. Vajra dance is the expression of inner freedom and awareness. It can invoke a powerful feeling of being liberated, shifting consciousness to release mental constraints. Many Chöd liturgies include vajra dance as a way of overpowering and subduing inner demons. It is associated with ecstatic awakening.

The concept of "vajra" is one of the most significant themes in tantric Buddhism. *Vajra* is a Sanskrit word meaning both "diamond" and "thunderbolt" and also refers to a ritual weapon with the properties of both. Like the thunderbolt, the vajra cleaves through ignorance. It is also used as an analogy to describe something that is indestructible and connotes something that is sacred. In the end, it does not describe anything that lies outside of ourselves. Instead, it points out the primordial essence of our being: that our true nature is unborn, deathless, and transcends all conditions.

At times, practitioners may have a spontaneous dance arise in them through the power of their joyful awakening. In Tibet there are many stories about extraordinary masters who got up and spontaneously danced in front of everybody. They made no announcement that dance was part of the ceremony or that a dance was on its way. They simply and suddenly danced as part of their spiritual experience in that moment, sometimes in the middle of their teaching. The renowned lama, Khenpo Jigme Phuntsok, who passed away in 2004, would sometimes get up and do a vajra dance in front of thousands of people. His spontaneous dance was understood by everyone to be the pure expression of the joy of his inner awakening.

Before I met Khenpo Jigme Phuntsok personally, I was part of a group who received an initiation to do Manjushri practice from him. After the empowerment, I went to meet him, and he looked like a mountain sitting in front of me—like an impressive, giant, mountain-like monk. At first, I was overwhelmed by his great presence and moved by his enormous spirit. I had the sense of myself being insignificant. When he started talking, he was pouring love and compassion out to me, even though I had never met him before. He gave me deep heart advice, not just Buddhist philosophy but meaningful guidance. Like a kind and great uncle giving me loving assistance, he guided me on my path. I once saw a picture of him dancing a vajra dance and could see how ecstatic he was inside. He was just like the ancient Buddhist masters who expressed their inner freedom and love through improvisational dance. It would be inspiring to have more masters doing joyful dance in our world, to wake us up to unconditional freedom and break through our silly concepts and ideas.

In Chöd liturgies, visualization infuses the vajra dance with a flavor of power, joy, and fearless confidence. In some parts of the liturgy, we witness dakinis dancing on the heads of inner poisons, and in others we become the female deity Vajrayogini, one of the most beloved figures in Tibetan iconography. She represents the essence of transcendent passion, free of selfishness and illusion, skillfully destroying ego-clinging. Many Indian and Tibetan tantrikas embrace her as their most beloved deity. Often, she appears as red in color, sometimes peaceful and sometimes wrathful. She is popular in both the old and new tantric schools of Tibetan Buddhism, representing inner freedom, great emptiness, and the dharmakaya. In *The Dakini's Laughter*, the first visualization is of ourselves as a giant Vajrayogini holding a skin bag in her right hand and trumpet in her left, dancing ecstatically.

When practitioners prepare for the dance, we invite in the enlightened guests, including the masters of our lineage. We then imagine that the five dakinis are dancing on the heads of demons that are symbolic representations of inner poisons. We may also be moved to get up and dance, using traditional choreography or spontaneous and inspired movements as a way of conquering the inner poisons. The dance is accompanied by the music of a bell and drum, along with singing the liturgy. Just imagining this allows an immediate shift in consciousness, so that we drop our ordinary ego identification and arise in the expanded consciousness. We are no longer the egoic personal self but are transformed through ritual into an indescribable, pure consciousness.

Vajra dances can be peaceful or wrathful, expressing the ecstasy of inner freedom and triumph and celebrating mastery over our inner poisons. Some dances were developed by masters through their visions of dakas and dakinis. *Daka* and *dakini* are Sanskrit for the Tibetan word *khandro*, meaning "sky dancer," a type of deity. The terms can refer to one of these deities or to a human being who is awakened by the tantric Buddhist path. They are archetypal male and female forms representing ecstatic, liberated mind. Even though many people associate the Tibetan word *khandro* with female entities, it is only female when it is in the form *khandroma*. The word *khandro* alone is gender neutral. It gives an image of a deity traveling in space beyond hinderances. But that is simply an analogy for enlightened mind that is free—no longer shackled by conflicting emotions.

In this practice, we create a mandala of five dakinis along with all enlightened masters and deities visualized in our minds. A mandala, discussed in detail in chapter 9, is a sacred configuration organized around a central unifying principle. It can refer to an assembly of deities or a gathering of tantrikas, or tantric practitioners. Tantrikas engage what is referred to as "the mandala principle" by creating sacred space either in relation to their immediate environment or by perceiving that their whole world is a sacred realm.

In this mandala, the space is filled with vivid yet transparent forms of enlightened dakas and dakinis in each of the cardinal directions including the center. Each direction has a specific dakini whose characteristics energetically resonate with that direction and relate to one of the five buddha families: the vajra, ratna, padma, karma, and buddha families. The white vajra dakini dances in the east; the yellow ratna dakini, in the south; the red padma dakini, in the west; the green karma dakini, in the north; and the blue buddha dakini, at the center of the mandala. Each holds a ritual implement and dances with joy while trampling on the heads of the archetypal demons and monsters—called *rakshasas, yama raja,* and so forth—residing in their specific cardinal direction.

This image may be shocking to those who are not familiar with such methodology, but though it may seem violent, it is not. First, these demonic forms are just archetypal representations of our neuroses—the five poisons, or kleshas. The dakinis are symbolically celebrating the subjugation of the army of maras and triumph over the five inner poisons. They are not dancing with hatred or with the intention to disparage or harm but rather with love, compassion, and profound wisdom. Therefore, the dance is powerful and playful at the same time. When we maintain awareness and are grounded in the meditative state of samadhi, a spontaneous inspiration to dance during practice can help us release internal blockage and experience spontaneity and joy. We dance freely, ecstatically, and in utter liberation—which is the meaning of "sky dancer," dakini.

The practice of visualization is not intended to replace ordinary experience with a hallucinatory model or to become a spiritual bypass for our daily life activities. But rather, we cultivate—through continued, skillful, and guided practice—familiarity with the limitless dimension of mind. This complex visualization expresses all dimensions of mind in its natural, liberated state. Its force cracks open the practitioner's habitual mind, allowing us to touch into the dynamic nature of unconditioned reality.

The five dakinis each represent one of the five wisdoms, which are aspects of enlightened mind. They wear symbolic ornaments and crowns, and their colors are vivid, intense, and magnificent yet transparent. Their forms can be imagined like rainbow light—with form and color but insubstantial—just as light radiates from a sunlit crystal or a rainbow appears in the sky. Since they are energetic forms, like light, they have no physicality—no intestines, blood, or bones like solid forms.

In the east, the white vajra dakini represents mirror-like wisdom, which is the ability to perceive the whole of reality—sights, sounds, touch, taste, and thoughts—without any egoic desire to hold on to them. This wisdom sees that their nature is illusory, transient, and empty of any solid, intrinsic reality. Just like the images flow across a mirror's surface and the mirror does not hold on to them, all images are transitory. Mirror-like wisdom is that aspect of enlightened mind that is able to clearly perceive reality yet not conceptualize it.

In the south, the yellow ratna dakini represents the wisdom of equality, which is enlightened mind experiencing the whole of reality without judgement or preferences and seeing the intrinsic nature of all things as the same. All divisions, separations, and duality are merely mental constructs imposed by the ego. Any experience or object is not holier or better than any other; they are equal in their true nature.

In the west, the red padma dakini represents the discriminating awareness aspect of wisdom mind. Free of all dualism, there is tremendous openness without separation. But being nonconceptual does not mean it is a dull state where nothing is happening— it involves skillful actions, compassion, and inquisitiveness. Its implement of compassion is a sharp blade of loving discernment, which is intelligent in comprehending the complex nature of reality. This sharp intelligence sees things and their idiosyncratic characteristics clearly.

In the north, the green karma dakini represents all-accomplishing wisdom, which is the aspect of enlightened mind that is wise, sublime, and has the potency to complete all actions. It is utterly creative and dynamic and can motivate itself. Its energy is to engage with the world and do things to help others with whatever means are necessary. It is dynamic—not stagnant. With meticulous effort, it employs whatever means necessary to help the world in every situation. This dakini represents the wisdom of all-accomplishment as an energetic force that motivates action in the world through love, courage, and compassion.

In the center, the blue buddha dakini represents the wisdom of dharmata, or the wisdom-ground of all. Dharmata is the naked, unconditioned truth, the nature of reality, the true nature of phenomenal existence. It represents the enlightened mind that is awakened to emptiness—all-pervading space, the nondual nature of all things—without the slightest wave of delusion. This is the quintessence of all the other wisdoms.

In *The Dakini's Laughter*, these dakinis dance on the heads of the five kleshas—the inner poisons or conflicting emotions—represented in the form of demonic figures. If we grasp or identify with them, they will obstruct awakening and incite us to unwholesome actions. Each dakini has a specific ability to skillfully conquer one of the five kleshas: vajra dakini conquers hatred, ratna dakini overcomes the obstacle of pride, padma dakini vanquishes desire, karma dakini tramples jealousy, and the buddha dakini accomplishes bodhicitta by vanquishing ignorance.

Many cultures use demons as psychological scapegoats, projecting all negativities, evils, fears, and misfortune onto them. Some have developed practices of exorcism and believe that evil can be kicked out from our system and society through these ceremonies. There are also ceremonies in Tibetan culture that have an outward appearance of exorcism. But Tibetan ceremonies do not kick evil out of the participants but liberate us from the inner poisons of ego. When we practice Chöd or any other tantric Buddhist sadhana, it is important to remember this description and the significance of these five dakinis. Without this true meaning, it could become a mere hallucination with no transformative impact.

It is crucial to remember that though we call inner poisons "demons," they are archetypal, allegorical representations of our neuroses and are not to be regarded as a real entity. Images of evil forces show up in all cultures. For example, in Western culture, jealousy is anthropomorphized as a green-eyed monster in order to point out how poisonous it can be. It is also a way to depict how jealousy functions: once unleashed, it becomes a monster that causes great pain and cannot be easily controlled. It can lead us to unwholesome actions, such as putting down someone else's glory through backbiting and ignoble schemes to destroy them. Someone who grew up in a superstitious culture could associate these demons as real evil, malevolent supernatural beings from outside, but this would be a big pitfall. Rather, by making internal negative forces visible—by illustrating them in sacred art forms and in sacred ceremony—we become more conscious of them. They can then be more easily uprooted.

These demons are ubiquitous archetypes in Tibetan culture: the Tibetan people have a clear understanding of the idiosyncrasies of each demon. While they may seem exotic to non-Tibetans, they help the practitioner understand hang-ups and obstructing forces and shed the light of awareness on them. English too has a lot of ways to describe the felt sense of these forces, such as someone being "green with envy," "bloated with pride," or "boiling with rage." Even though we say these things casually, they precisely convey the emotional energy. Through these phrases and images, we are reminded that these disruptive forces can destroy our peace of mind and sense of well-being. Naming our neuroses—identifying them with archetypal images and language—can be a potent method to uncover how we are affected by them and to clearly identify what they are. It can be a way of bringing to light the dark places within us. It becomes a benevolent psychology when done with love and compassion.

At the inception of Western psychology, when these forces were first being explored, named, and recognized as obstructive patterns, there was a tendency to reduce human experience into a myriad of diagnostic codes. By emphasizing what was wrong, psychology and neuroscience took an approach of "find and fix."

More recent developments in the field of psychology have come closer to the view of tantric Buddhism, which sees inner negative forces as transformable energetic states and not intrinsically bad. Buddhism emphasizes transforming neuroses through love and wisdom. Chöd views human consciousness as free of conditions, as pure awareness, or buddha nature. All of our inner poisons are incidental to that. Their nature is the display of our consciousness, which we should not be attached to. Tantric Buddhism teaches that the nature of everything that exists, including our neuroses, is sacred, and that our true nature is already perfect from the beginning. We work with neuroses in the spirit of love, acceptance, compassion, and playfulness. The vajra dance skillfully releases our neuroses in the most playful and ecstatic way.

These images of dakinis dancing on the heads of inner obstacles portrayed as monstrous beings could be misunderstood as aggressive, but they are not. Rather, we imagine that the dakinis are playful, full of love and compassion, and are having a good time—almost partying. In our best moments of self-awareness, we may find humor in our idiosyncrasies and gently laugh at ourselves. Can you imagine meeting your deepest, lifelong inner obstacles with love? Can you imagine accepting your most troublesome inner negative forces so completely that they are transformed and you become free from acting them out and causing grief?

Suffering is cut when we have compassion toward our shadow and neuroses, when we are able to see them not as some separate thing but as an integral, lively part of us. These contorted dimensions of experience are not an alien species or mental virus occupying part of our system. They are part of us. They should not be hated, because then we would be hating ourselves, which is a form of violence. In that spirit, we completely embrace human neuroses, knowing that they are not intrinsically bad but are part of the whole human experience. These are the powerful negative forces frozen by ego, sometimes stagnated, that then become a source of suffering.

Someone might imagine spirituality to be a form of biting the lip, becoming a sort of spiritual soldier facing a formidable enemy within. From this place, it may seem that there is a long arduous journey ahead before achieving any relief from suffering. Some might imagine that countless hours of analysis and self-discipline are required to purify obstacles. Tantra, and especially Chöd, is the opposite of this. Our friendly and gentle attitude is everything. By facing the obstacles of lifelong inner poisons and suffering, they readily release under the profound implements of love, compassion, joy, and equanimity.

The five poisons are directly correlated with the five wisdoms. They are experienced differently, but their fundamental nature is the same. This is because they are all empty, with no ground and no root. This can be regarded as a nondual psychology. Once transformed through skillful means and wisdom, these negative forces become unobstructed expressions of the colorful play of phenomena and no longer bind our consciousness. The king of demons associated with hatred or anger is transformed by love into vajra wisdom. The yama raja, the lord of death epitomizing pride, is transformed through compassion into ratna wisdom. The *rakshasi*, the cannibal of desire, is transformed by joy into padma wisdom. The demon of jealousy is transformed by equanimity into karma wisdom. The *shidré*, or ghosts of the dead, which induce ignorance, awaken into bodhicitta, the enlightened mind. In the view of nonduality, poison and wisdom have the same essence.

There are also scientific clues to this nondual outlook. The big bang started from one atom and exploded into this infinite universe, giving birth to stars. Then a supernova occurred and created stardust, which we are all made from. From this place of nonduality, we can appreciate the sacred interdependence of all living beings. We can not say that anything is intrinsically bad or good. We no longer perceive our inner poisons as wrong or demonic. We experience them as the same as anything else, and the inner bondage is released. This process is unique because many psychological and religious disciplines engage in the context of struggle, effort, and endless analysis to declare a holy war on these forces. I like to use the term *forces* for our fears and emotions, because the heavy-handed judgement and dualism is no longer there: they are simply transient inner forces. This is very freeing.

Within some tantric practices, we work with these forces by intensifying the five inner poisons deliberately. This helps us learn to be with the intensified version of desire or jealousy, to witness them and recognize them as empty, with no ground and no root. In this way, we can experience powerful liberation from them, suddenly severing the inner cord that binds us to them. At this moment our ego identity opens into that which is nameless. We arise in an egoless state of consciousness and are immediately in touch with the best version of ourselves—fearless, wise, courageous.

Though there are many different traditions within the Abrahamic religions, they all tend to have principal differences from Eastern nontheistic traditions. Some of the more esoteric sects may share deep wisdom and openness with Buddhism, but the fundamental difference is Buddhism's nondual view. The underpinnings of theistic dualism generally regard transcendent states as separate from ordinary life. In Eastern religions, good and evil are not exclusive, because duality is transcended. The Buddha is not a divine terminator, and we are not fighting against evil. Evil cannot take us over and deceive or prompt us to misbehave. The attitude toward darkness is not from heavy-handed judgement but from acceptance and realizing that darkness is an integral part of life. D. T. Suzuki, a renowned Zen Buddhist teacher, was once asked about Western religion, and he famously replied, "God against man. Man against God. Man against nature. Nature against man. Nature against God. God against nature. Very funny religion!"

Even though all of our conflicting emotions show up in a demonic form in the vajra dance, demons are not "bad" as they might be in Abrahamic traditions. We should always bear this in mind and not bring bias from our ancestral religious concepts. Those who grew up in this tantric Buddhist view tend to understand the nondual outlook. But even for us, the understanding can be philosophical, and we may still find it difficult to embrace the outlook in actual experience. We all have deep-seated dualism in our subconscious.

There are two unique methods for how to work with neuroses in tantric Buddhism. The first is transformation, or *gyur* in Tibetan. This means that enlightenment is not about rejecting inner poisons but is a state of not being bound by them. This method has to do with metaphorically transforming the five poisons into the five wisdoms. This sounds like alchemy, in the sense that we are transforming ourselves in unimaginable ways. The tantras recommend deliberately enhancing poisons, such as desire, then visualizing ourselves as deities in the same moment. From this state, we can simply witness the desire, without grasping the energy, until we are no longer bound by it, even though the energy of it is still present. In that moment, liberating awakening takes place without any struggle. The notion of transformation is nondual in itself. It allows for energetically sensing that these forces are not enemies, that the energy of desire and the object of desire are not separate. Then transformation can work.

The other method is actually doing nothing at all, because there is no need to demonize or reject inner poisons, their nature being empty pure awareness. All this requires is simply looking into their nature when they arise. In such a moment, we can see that the nature of the poisons are not different than anything else. They have no solid ground and are just floating forces. The power of looking into them immediately stops our urge to do something with them. Looking into them on the spot—seeing their true nature as groundless and rootless—gives us the sense that there is nothing to grasp, nothing to hold on to. This gives us the ability to be free of them immediately. They liberate themselves. This second method is called *shé*, which means "understanding" and refers to the realization that the nature of all forces in our system is empty and luminous, with no ground and no root. Both approaches have a nondual basis. Our way to enlightenment is not through a holy war of good against evil, but through recognizing the nature of all things and dancing with the joy of that realization. In this way, all experiences become fertilizer for waking up.

6

Cutting Through in Everyday Life

When I started practicing Buddhism, I did not know so much about introspection. I simply practiced to accumulate merit. I practiced with the idea that if I recited mantra and liturgy, my merit, or punya, was being gathered somewhere. Once I started studying more, I began to understand the categories of inner poisons and that gave me a whole new level of insight. I realized that the true purpose of Buddhist practice is to become aware of and purify my own destructive emotions. This was a paradigm shift for me and changed the very nature of my spiritual practice. Spiritual disciplines not only elevate our spiritual life but also impact how we regard our ordinary life and the world around us. If we invest days, hours, weeks into learning to perfect a formal practice such as Chöd but at the end of retreat plunge back headlong into confusion, then the practice has been for nothing.

Integrating profound and esoteric teachings into every day life is what makes them meaningful. I tell my students to allow the inspiration and essence of Chöd to infuse their consciousness and stay in the forefront of their minds. This is how they can carry Chöd practice as a journey rather than an occasional spiritual observance.

What is required to practice Chöd in everyday life is awareness. In this context, awareness is a state of intentional observation that monitors what is happening in our consciousness. It does not have to be strenuous. We do not have to be an awareness marathon athlete. This awareness is observant but at ease and nonjudgmental. It can be relaxed and easy. There is a way we can gently observe and see what is going on in our minds continuously. This rests on our ability to catch ourselves whenever the inner demons come out, so that we are not at their mercy. Its basis is a psycho-spiritual development of recognizing our inner demons.

Those who have never done such reflection may suspect that it will not be fun to look into their own minds. They think that all they may discover is the messiness of boredom, worry, or resentment, which they typically avoid by any means possible. Ego has an avoidance strategy, which is to keep the thinking mind occupied with itself by continually churning with busy thoughts and indulging itself in entertainment. When people begin to make the effort to become aware of themselves, their thoughts, and emotions, there is a danger of awareness becoming too tight. They start judging themselves and become uncomfortable. They become self-conscious and rigid, which can prevent them from going along with the flow of life. On the other hand, people sometimes choose not to become aware of themselves, because part of them is unconsciously resistant to becoming enlightened.

The Scottish psychiatrist R. D. Laing said that we are all afraid of three things: people, our own minds, and death. Often when people first practice meditation they feel afraid of their own minds. Sitting and being with their minds can easily cause frustration, boredom, anxiety, and anger to come out. On top of that, they experience a heightened awareness that can be shocking. They may feel naked, embarrassed, or that everyone can energetically read what is going on in their minds. It is very uncomfortable to feel so exposed to the world. As we learn to be with our own minds, more subtle levels of awareness emerge, allowing us to see the most subtle levels of mind's internal habits. We begin to realize that practice is not just about gathering merit but is about true introspection and uprooting old habitual patterns.

Along the way, awareness may show up as the experience of being mortified by how much is still left to go. This is a good sign, because if we do not get mortified with all that goes on in the mind, we can get complacent. In this way, being embarrassed can help us return to awareness with even stronger commitment. Watching the mind can be boring, but it can also be wild and full of conflict. The vortex of negative thoughts, guilt, fear, loneliness, complaint, and anxiety can go on for a long time in the beginning. We do not have to go far to find the inner demons in our consciousness. They are there, and in moments of being alone without distraction, whole armies of them will show up.

Buddhist meditation encourages us to be with the rawness of our minds, not to run away or manipulate. Meditation is nonjudgmental: what shows up is noticed with neutrality and eventually dissolves. The point of cultivating awareness is to develop an ability to welcome whatever shows up with a nonjudgmental attitude. What you are seeing would no longer cause anxiety, embarrassment, or discomfort. In awareness there is the freedom of being able to witness whatever is unfolding without taking it personally. Eventually, in moments, you may feel that you are an indescribable pure awareness: that all emotions and experience are no longer you. You can cut through attachment and identification to them right away.

Traditional Buddhism presents and defines many levels of consciousness, but in general the hierarchy of human consciousness can be viewed as three levels of awareness. At the bottom level there is no conscience, no idea of right and wrong. In this place, there is no understanding of why love, compassion, courage, or enlightenment are important or of the impact of negative emotions. In this state, one cannot recognize what results in harm or benefit. This leads to various degrees of acting out, misdeeds, and harming ourselves and others, including extreme examples such as sociopathy. While it may be hard to imagine someone with such a conscience, many movies and fiction stories portray characters who seem capable of doing unthinkable things to other people. We can imagine that such people in the world simply never had the right circumstances to evolve. Many conditions—such as growing up lacking compassionate role models or dealing with heavy karma—would lead someone to exist at the very bottom of the hierarchy of consciousness, where there is not even basic, rudimentary insight about what is good or bad. They may indulge in hatred without any idea that hating is unwholesome. They may even get some satisfaction from hating, or they may glorify it.

Once you move up on the hierarchy of consciousness, a sense of right and wrong, vice and virtue develops. This mental development leads people to become motivated to do good things and perhaps become religious. Becoming reasonable, decent, and moral, they may turn away from violence and causing pain to others. It is still possible, however, to lack self-reflection and only behave in the manner prescribed by a moral dogma. They lead life from a scripture, holy book, or secularly defined value system that outlines a sense of right and wrong but lacks authentic inward investigation and self-reflection.

As consciousness develops further, people begin to have their own intelligence and deep wisdom about right and wrong. They are able to allow the natural expression of innate compassion and wisdom not based on acquired knowledge from outside or moral prescriptions. By being more self-reflective, they begin to see, and become repulsed by, the not-so-holy things they find in their minds. Initially this can be a judgmental experience, where we are embarrassed about ourselves, and nervous, becoming our own harshest critic. Even though this is painful, it indicates that our consciousnesses are evolving.

Ultimately, the highest level of inner maturity is a state of consciousness where you are fully aware of all of your thoughts, opinions, emotions, and inner poisons. Seeing these qualities of mind does not create internal conflict. There is deep knowing and acceptance that these are part of being human, and you see yourself with compassionate wisdom. You are able to rouse bodhicitta, rest in awareness, and see through these conflicts. You are not bound by them and do not need to act on them. Rather, your whole consciousness is drawn toward loving compassion. Chöd is based on the nonjudgement that is awareness from the highest level of consciousness. From that place, even though we are calling these negative elements "inner demons," we are actually welcoming and feeding them, throwing a party for them. With awareness, we go inward to identify neuroses, and rather than being tormented by their psychological collateral damage, we embrace them as offerings.

Through practice we begin to realize the interdependent effects these states of mind have on ourselves and on the world. Imagine someone who is grouchy all the time. That person may not abuse anyone verbally, but just being with them can create lots of friction and bring everyone down energetically. We begin to recognize that these powerful inner demons can hold us back.

Identifying them clearly and working on them one by one, examining how they affect us and others, is the insight of Chöd.

Each individual has a unique journey in this regard. As we evolve, our awareness becomes more astute. You may realize that this year, you must work on fear, which may be a whole new issue from last year. You home in on how it influences your life and poisons your relationships. Having worked with fear, the next year may present something else that is holding you back in other ways. Clearly identifying inner demons and regularly creating new assignments for our own introspection can direct our conscious evolution. It requires humility to recognize the blind spots in which we can fool ourselves.

A group of friends in Austin, Texas, once took me to hear live country music. I had not listened to live country music before, and they wanted to share this with me. We were in a large restaurant, and it seemed that most people were regular customers who knew each other. Seeing someone she knew, my friend introduced me to a lady sitting nearby saying, "This is Anam Thubten. Tomorrow he's giving a talk on meditation. Would you like to come?" The lady responded by declaring, "No, I'm pretty evolved already." She could have been totally right! But true humility means not fantasizing that through this process of becoming aware of your patterns, you have become enlightened. Humility means not telling yourself a beautiful story that you are enlightened or that you don't need to look inside, even though everyone else does. It means not letting yourself believe that you are the greatest yogi in your neighborhood, saying to yourself, "I'm pretty evolved."

In each day, the moment we wake up, we are interacting with and in relation to the world. There is no way of knowing whether the world will be kind that day, push your buttons, or do everything that will make you happy. We have no assurance that the universe is doing everything in accordance with our wishes and preferences. Sometimes days begin and the first moment of walking into the kitchen we find the coffee machine broken. What do we do? This is the first test, the first moment when we can lose our cool completely by reacting, becoming upset, and trying to find someone to blame. Conversely, we can notice the rising frustration and let it go. Maybe we wake up with lots of pain in our body, muscle spasms making it difficult to walk. Or, we may run into someone on the street and have an unpleasant encounter. Anything can happen. Each day our experience oscillates between the world being kind and being rough. Little and big events are constantly triggering our inner demons. There are moments, opportunities, where they can rule us or where we can apply methods to be free from them.

Our internal suffering does not really require any external stimulus to come into being. These patterns tend to repeat by themselves. A perfect evening in your living room—comfortable on the couch after a nice dinner—can be interrupted by a thought out of nowhere. Before you know it, your whole being can be in the grips of worry, whether rational or not. Many of our thoughts are not rational even though we allow them to take over our consciousness. For example, worry is painful and can become a chronic mental disease that our ego keeps feeding on. Mark Twain said, "I have had lots of worries in my life, most of which never happened." Even if our worrying is sometimes rational, there is a way we can be wiser in our choices or have more discernment rather than allowing worry to destroy our peace of mind. One way to do that is to remind ourselves that the things we worry about do not necessarily happen.

Our suffering perpetuates itself without the need of external stimulus. If it is not worry occupying our minds, it could be anger or something else. The ego always finds a way to continue suffering. Often people allow themselves to react strongly because they have not trained in the spiritual practice of equanimity. Whereas with practice, you can live in awareness and whenever those binding thoughts arise from external stimulus, you can cut through the energetic binding and not react. As we practice Chöd in everyday life, we find increased freedom, have more choice to stay in equilibrium and are less reactive than in the past.

Exciting breakthroughs in consciousness can happen as the result of well-disciplined daily meditation practice or after retreat. The effect of retreat can stay with us, but just as often, the bliss and inspiration of intensive practice subsides after we return to daily life, leaving us with a sense that nothing has been released or purified. This can be disappointing, and many people struggle with it. People who come to my retreats occasionally ask my advice about these ebbs and flows, concerned that they may be missing the point or need to find a new, more lasting spiritual technique. What I find is that people underestimate the deep commitment needed for a lifelong path of practice. Because of this, people do not have complete vigilance to apply the practices in everyday life, in every moment.

If you view your life as an opportunity for everyday life practice, you will find the inspiration, the inner force, needed to keep you from getting stuck. You will be able to bring everything to the path of practice, meeting all life events with an open heart and with love, not reacting but rather integrating challenging experiences with the commitment that is required. In this way, you do not let anything go as an ordinary, unconscious response but rather bring it all to practice. Our obstructing habits can die, but it takes continual and diligent commitment to transform them.

Sometimes the effort seems too challenging. A friend told me a story about a painful rift with her siblings. Though they were not on speaking terms, she dedicated her practice to them for years and sent many good wishes and prayers their way, hoping to somehow open communications and express the love in her heart so they could receive it. But nothing seemed to work. She was unaware of the pride she took in how "good" she had been through her dedications and still felt the others were to blame for the rift in communication. When she shared this story with her teacher, he asked a few questions, and my friend tearfully explained how much she had done. At some point, her teacher leaned forward and gently but bluntly said, "Well, you haven't done enough." My friend was shocked but quickly realized how her pride had gotten in the way, and the real change had to happen internally, not in her siblings. Transformation was possible after that, and eventually they all began speaking to each other again.

Another common example of letting our habits die is being cut off while driving on the highway. Though people have unique difficulties in life, this seems to be a universal challenge, so I use it with humor. We can bring everything into the context of practice. If you are driving and do not have the context of this philosophy of bringing everything into practice, you could react and get angry. But if you bring every situation into the paradigm of Chöd, you can think, "I will embrace this moment right away to sever my angry reaction." Applying the practice every moment helps us navigate the whole day in the most skillful way. Getting cut off in traffic, we can wish the other driver well or thank them for slowing us down. If anger or frustration arises, let it be. Do not act out by screaming or honking.

It is not as if every time you confront a difficult stimulus from outside that you must conduct a whole ceremony. Even yogis sometimes use simple methods when they are dealing with conflicting emotions and difficulties. They may not do the whole liturgy but sometimes simply exclaim the syllable *phet*. This is the most important syllable in the Chöd teachings. Even in Machig Labdrön's writing, *phet* is mentioned both as an aphorism and the mantra of Chöd. The simple techniques like mantras or exclamations of a syllable, or chants, or a yogic posture can help us to have this inner release. These methods do not carry some intrinsic power, but they help us enhance our intention to be free. They also help shatter the buildup of energetic clouds of thoughts and emotions, making them collapse.

Even in a secular sense, there are ways we can begin to work with our minds using self-liberating techniques. I know a wonderful couple who are farmers in Wyoming. I would never imagine that they would get into conflict with each other as they are such pure spirits, earth-loving, on the edge of society, working hard, and living a non-materialistic, alternative lifestyle. But they surprised me once by telling me that they had made up their own mudra to cut through conflict. When they feel tension, they use what they call the kitty cat mudra to restore their shared, loving sense of humor. One or the other will raise their hands like cat's paws, using this gesture to break the story line and tension between them. Most often it makes them laugh. The moment they laugh, the angry energy is cut on the spot. When they told me this, it really seemed like "Chöd on the spot," bringing a profound ancient practice into an ordinary situation.

Cutting through stagnant energy can actually be an easy job. The attitude needed here is of embracing and accepting obstacles, not treating them as evil or neurotic but as interesting forces within us. All we are doing is simply melting the frozen energy rather than continuing to wall it off and reject it. This approach takes divine confidence—excellent, delightful confidence—rather than a strained, jaw-gripping effort to uproot stuck places in us. When we let go of struggling against a powerful force, relax the effort to bend it to our will, and adopt an attitude of joyous confidence, this easily results in purifying old patterns. We can fearlessly play with them, no longer captured by any outer or inner force. When conflict arises in your mind, try adopting an attitude of "easy peasy" by starting in a place of compassion. Then, drop the complaint.

Chöd is based on the profound realization that inner poisons are fundamentally not bad and not permanent but are simply energies or forces that do not have solid, immutable characteristics. They seem very solid when perpetuated by our unawareness, but emotions do not have a fixed character. They have a flowing energy. They do not get stagnant on their own but become stagnant first through unawareness. Often our tendency is to indulge in them instead of releasing them. When we indulge in them, they do not just flow through us but become trapped in our systems and begin to rule our minds. Confusion and suffering follow. The nature of emotions is to be fleeting experiences, but because we lack this view, we suffer from believing they are real. Once we believe the validity of an initial thought, it gives rise to an emotion, and from that, solid stories about reality are born.

Story lines are just a fabrication of our minds, which do not really correspond to the nature of reality. It is easier to release our thoughts and emotions when we abide in the insight of emptiness. In Chöd and Dzogchen practice, there is an important notion known as "no ground and no root," or *zhimé tsadral*. When this notion is applied to our inner poisons, then all human experience, all conflicting experiences, can be seen as empty appearance. When we look directly into them, the ground upon which they show up is not really there. By looking directly, one sees there is no root from which they arise. Instead, they are flowing, transient forces within the mind. They are there and not there. The ground they depend on is not supported, like a house with no foundation. They will not be there in the next few seconds, because they have no lifespan. If you do not hold on to them, they can be transformed instantly and dissolved because there is no ground and no root.

Such experience of thoughts and emotions flowing through you often happens during meditation. If someone is a well-seasoned meditator, this is not far-fetched but is completely relatable and can be witnessed directly. Thoughts and emotions arise, dwell, then dissolve. They are not intrinsically good, or bad, or permanent. They have no definitive characteristics. Once we experience cutting the root of thoughts and emotions, we may try to hang on to the feeling of being freed from them. Then we may try to make that feeling solid. This can lead to feeling righteous about having had the experience. Since the experience of freedom and the sense of righteousness need to be cut, even the most beautiful and profound experiences that arise in meditation should be welcomed, but one should not be attached to them. Otherwise, once again our minds will feel that our experiences do have ground and root. When that happens, we have to reenter the path of awareness and remind ourselves all over again what we are committing to and why.

Chöd is a path of self-liberation. By awakening ourselves, we are not relying on supernatural phenomena. There is no Chöd god who deals with our inner obstacles for us. The secret of this whole path is to commit to awakening, commit to cutting through. The Chödpas I encounter in Tibet who identify themselves as lifelong Chöd practitioners must make a strong commitment, like being married to the path. It is very serious, and they do not take the path lightly. Their commitment comes from the bottom of their hearts. Anyone committed to developing awareness, metaphorically, has to get married to the path. You have to commit to be on the path all the time, in times of joy and sorrow. Once you turn awareness into a lifelong path, the commitment will be established in your consciousness and heart. It becomes a direction and force in your life that you will be able to remember every day. That's the idea.

PART TWO

CHÖD IN PRACTICE

7

Refuge

Due to not understanding that this uncontrived, self-
arisen awareness
is the true refuge,
living beings drown in the ocean of suffering.
Please give them refuge in the awakened mind of the
three kayas.

—*The Dakini's Laughter*

Each Chöd tradition has its own refuge mandala, a set of figures
to whom the practitioner takes refuge. In *The Dakini's Laughter* liturgy, the central visualized figure is the primordial Buddha,
Vajradhara, who is considered the lord of all buddhas. His color is
blue like the sky, representing the realm of reality, or dharmata,
the nature of everything that is vast and all pervasive. He is surrounded by an assembly of wisdom beings, buddhas, *ishtadevatas*
(a practitioner's favorite deity), and *vidyadharas* (wisdom holders). In Buddhist practice, we take refuge in the Buddha, embracing the wisdom being as a guide; in the Dharma as the path; and
in the Sangha, or community, as companions on our journey.

Chöd practice includes an inner, unconditioned refuge, which is our buddha nature—the primordial Buddha, the wisdom of awakening, the unconditioned. But what does it mean to take refuge? Taking refuge is not necessarily an idea that comes up in everyday life. However, in times of danger, people escaping from social unrest or natural disasters immediately seek something to take refuge in and are called refugees. They may have a sense of seeking sanctuary and protection under the grace of whatever benevolent individual, institution, or country they can find. But ordinarily we do not speak about or consider taking refuge. Nonetheless, we are always taking refuge in something without even knowing it. Usually unconsciously, we take refuge in things such as relationships, money, or physical and mental comforts. These refuges give us a sense of being OK and safe. Even though we do not put it into a conceptual framework, that is what we are doing. These habits do not, however, provide real happiness. Rather, they deceive us and become obstacles to spiritual growth.

Human beings have a longing for security, certainty, and for their lives to make sense. Without this, they may feel fearful and anxious and that their existence is resting on rickety ground. Humans do everything in their power to create a sense of security for themselves and for their loved ones. We devote almost every aspect of human society to creating and maintaining security. This has been true all along from the beginning of history. Even prior to human written history, which is only five thousand years old, our ancestors, no matter how primitive, did everything to have security. Sometimes the driving force in our lives is to create this sense of security for ourselves. If we are doing enough to achieve this goal, then we are regarded as functional, decent, respectable members of society.

In more primitive cultures people had some sort of wealth, not money in the bank or the stock market, but they gathered food in summer, and accumulated and stored grains or dried meat. They accumulated livestock and perhaps precious gems. Human communities, institutions, and relationships are created to feel secure but can collapse because their nature is transient. People are willing to take refuge in any random thing, even though what they have just taken refuge in turns out to be undependable and will soon leave them, resulting in disappointment and despair. What really challenges people is not having anything that feels like a ground for themselves.

Deep down, however, we know that all things we take refuge in for happiness or security are not permanent or reliable. But if that knowingness is always only on the surface—if we do not make friends with it—the discomfort will torment us. This is why people often use suppression and denial to cover such discomfort. We often treat troublesome facts of life, such as death, as taboo. Some cultures do not talk about death around the dinner table. We act as if we are going to live forever. We get serious about mundane affairs and get attached to little glories, even though subconsciously we know none of us will live forever. Sometimes such awakening comes to us when we are dying, but this may be too late. If we had this recognition ahead of time, we may have been able to have deeper peace in our hearts and would not have struggled as much.

For many people, belief in God provides promise, hope for this life, and a perspective on eternity. Yet, some people can lose faith in God, causing a huge crisis in them. This loss brings about doubts over the meaning of life and their place in the world. Once, while participating in a conference in the Santa Cruz Mountains in Northern California, a participant asked to speak to me about something personal. He shared with me that he was in a spiritual crisis because he had lost faith in God. At first, I could not understand the crisis, because as a Buddhist there would be no problem with losing faith in God. But I put myself in his shoes, began to empathize with his pain, and consoled him. What he lost faith in was a stereotypical Judeo-Christian, wrathful, male God. I was confident that this loss of faith would lead him to a deeper and nondual understanding of God. As time went by, he started coming to my teachings and attended several meditation retreats. We became good friends. Through his journey he found his own path, as well as peace of mind. He became a sincere Buddhist meditator.

Religious people, even Buddhists, may feel that they have someone they can take refuge in as a personal savior. This gives a tremendous sense of security and comfort. Yet, if you look closely, the notion of a personal savior does not exist in Buddhism. It is amazing that anyone ever came to listen to the teachings of Gautama Buddha, because from the start he declared that nobody can really save you. His central message was that you must free yourself. What he taught is counterintuitive to ego's desire for security. While taking refuge is a central aspect of Buddhism, it does not represent a personal savior outside of yourself—quite the opposite. It is a declaration to completely change your way of life through your own effort.

When someone wants to enter the Buddhist path, the initial step is to take refuge. The process involves taking a formal ceremonial vow in the presence of a monk, nun, or other master. Refuge in Buddhism is as much about what you *do not* take refuge in as what you *do* take refuge in. It is a vow to stop taking refuge in material sources of security, acknowledging that none of them are permanent and that they cannot grant you the highest freedom. Along with that, the person takes a list of subsidiary vows, such as nonviolence. The idea of taking refuge may sound as though we are desperate, hopeless, dispirited, and weak, but it is the other way around. Taking refuge provides a sense of courageous self-reliance. We become empowered through ceasing to take refuge in external illusions. We turn inward to find the highest truth.

Traditionally, Buddhists take refuge in the Three Jewels—Buddha, Dharma, and Sangha. This is the most standard refuge vow commitment. It means that we see the Buddha as an example, the Dharma as teachings, and the Sangha, or community, as companions. The Three Jewels are not just another ledge to step on, another rope that we can hold on to, or a more powerful version of God. Taking refuge must be done carefully and with the right understanding. It is not simply one ceremonial act but is a practice to be done in everyday life. This is why Tibetan Buddhist liturgies often begin with a verse on taking refuge. Many Buddhists recite a verse on refuge early in the morning every day to remind themselves of their vow and make it firm in their minds.

I am always inspired when people take refuge ordination, and I have offered the ceremony to many people over the last few decades. Over time, I adjusted how I conduct the ceremony. In the 1970s some Buddhist teachers began a trend of giving spiritual names during refuge vow ceremonies. I followed this trend as well in the early 2000s. It seemed like a cool thing to do. I had a refuge ceremony kit that contained a nice pair of scissors, a beautiful calligraphy pen, and my chop, or personal stamp. Whenever people took refuge, we clipped their hair and they received a refuge name written out in fine calligraphy with my chop on it. For the time being, I have stopped offering names during the refuge ceremony. This is partly because there is a limited variety of names and I found I was recycling them, giving them less meaning. I also did not want to inadvertently create a "spiritual badge" that people would hold on to. It seems that people are often moved by taking refuge, and I hoped that in addition to their joy in the ceremony, they would remember the vow as a way to continue following their path and not as something special to bolster their own identities.

Taking the vow and getting a symbolic haircut are an invitation to *not* take refuge in anything in the mundane world. Taking refuge is not a religious conversion or just the next new thing. It is important to understand that there will be no person or thing that will look after you eternally. You have to set yourself free though your own efforts. This is why the Buddha said, "I show the path to liberation, but you must realize that liberation is up to you."

TAKING REFUGE IN THE BUDDHA

Buddha, meaning "awakened one," generally refers to the individual, Shakyamuni Buddha, and in the plural to all awakened beings. The word can mean different things at different levels of Buddhist practice. Many Buddhists do not really understand the true philosophy behind taking refuge in the Buddha. It means to take the Buddha as a sacred guide, as your teacher, and as a source of inspiration. On this journey, the Buddha is the one who can inspire us through embodying love and wisdom. The *Udanavarga*, an early Buddhist scripture attributed to the Buddha and his disciples, states that you are your own lord and protector. It proclaims that as your own lord and protector, no outside being can save you from delusion. Your freedom from samsara is in your own hands.

Some speak of an axial age, which spanned approximately 800 to 300 B.C.E., a period when, without any obvious contact between them, Eurasian cultures simultaneously developed striking new ways of thinking. Persia, India, China, and the Greco-Roman world all flourished with new religious and philosophical views. It is useful to view this period as a time during which many of history's greatest thinkers and philosophers were born, including the Buddha, Lao Tzu, Socrates, and Zoroaster. Though living in far-flung places and cultures, each contributed to profound changes in human consciousness. Whether historically factual or not, this view points to humanity's interconnected wisdom, which is not owned by any one culture or philosophy.

What Shakyamuni Buddha taught by breaking away from the brahmin religion of his birth was unprecedented. Laying undiscovered in the background of human consciousness, realizations such as his tend to emerge during times when spiritual, political, and social conditions are ripe for change. A few highly developed individuals often herald these movements by proclaiming radical changes in consciousness. These individuals are often the tip of the iceberg, beneath which human consciousness has already begun to evolve. This rare person is able to broadcast the truth that expresses this change. Masses of people tune in. That is what happened in the time of Shakyamuni Buddha. Even though his teachings radically challenged individual beliefs, thousands and thousands came to hear him teach, including brahmins and untouchables: he had students from all walks of life.

REFUGE IN DHARMA

When we take refuge in the Dharma, we are committing to understand the teachings of the Buddha and to practice the Buddhist teachings in our lives. Some regard the word *Dharma* as a synonym for Buddhism, but this limits its meaning. Buddhism is a spiritual tradition that developed at a certain time in India, while Dharma is the practice and path to inner freedom, to inner awakening. Dharma can take many forms not limited to one sect or set of doctrines. Various traditions interpret the idea of Dharma differently, but in the context of the Three Jewels, Dharma is the path to inner freedom in harmony with the teachings of the Buddha.

Sometimes the Dharma may be too abstract a concept to be captured in our minds, so a system can help us have clear insight into it. Therefore, the noble eightfold path is considered the path of Dharma, providing explicit directions for how to practice. On the other hand, Dharma is vast and ineffable. It cannot be easily captured in intellectual structures. If we approach Dharma like a manual from which we just follow a set of rules and doctrines, we miss its true meaning. Rather, it is a genuine spiritual practice that provides the means, inspiration, and methods for inner awakening.

Dharma is a key concept in many Eastern religions such as Hinduism, Buddhism, Jainism, Sikhism, and others. Though the Buddhist Dharma encompasses vast volumes of texts, covering detailed concepts, principles, duties, and laws, taking refuge in the Dharma simply means that we commit to travel the path to inner freedom and benevolence. When we take refuge in the Dharma, we live life in harmony with the teachings proclaimed by Shakyamuni Buddha.

REFUGE IN THE SANGHA

Sangha is the community of spiritually like-minded people who practice the Dharma, such as monastic communities or congregations of practicing lay Buddhists, who practice Dharma in the spirit of fellowship. In addition, the Mahayana tradition includes the idea of the *arya* Sangha, or the exalted Sangha, which refers to the great enlightened bodhisattvas referred to in the sutras, such as Avalokiteshvara and Manjushri. These are the bodhisattvas who have awakened to seeing the nature of reality, great emptiness. Though in some systems "Sangha" refers strictly to monastics, in the broader sense it also includes the lay community of practicing Buddhists, including dedicated meditators and yogis. For example, the ninth-century Tibetan emperor Ralpachen, a devout Buddhist king, patronized both the monastic and lay Buddhist communities, showing great reverence to both. This is often mentioned by Tibetan historians to support the idea that the lay community of practicing Buddhists is a bona fide Sangha. Sanghas include communities of yogis and tantric practitioners, including Chödpas, who often have long hair, wear white robes, and many of whom have families.

Sanghas inspire and support each other on the journey. There are monasteries and nunneries in many countries throughout Asia where Buddhism is still vibrant, as well as in Western countries. Many of these monastic communities welcome lay practitioners for periods of deep study and retreat and embrace them as noble friends. Sangha can be found almost anywhere. Our mobile society and the flourishing of Buddhism around the world means that there is always a community of practitioners to find companionship with. It is very inspiring to see this development.

As a whole, Sanghas collectively embody the teachings of the Buddha and provide an environment in which we can feel our spiritual practice is supported. Many people these days have vast networks of fellow practitioners—like a kind network around the world, without boundaries. Because human beings influence each other, engaging in community helps keep us on the right track. During the coronavirus pandemic, our lifestyles and behavior changed at every level. Almost every social group, including spiritual ones, could not get together any longer because of the lockdown. My Sangha has a temple in the San Francisco Bay Area where people get together once a week to practice meditation. We feel that we are a living community. When the pandemic hit, we could no longer come together, so we began using online platforms for our meditation retreats. The silver lining of the pandemic was that our global community began participating in many online events. From this we developed a sense of greater community, connecting with wonderful spiritual beings around the world.

Taking refuge in the Sangha means opening our hearts to receive positive influence from others. Of the many communities we belong to—such as family, friends, and coworkers—taking refuge in the Sangha goes beyond the search for security and belonging. Refuge in Sangha means we are committed to both being inspired by and inspiring others to practice the Dharma. Sangha creates a container in which we can bring ordinary issues like jealousy, competition, shame, love, and passion into a meaningful perspective for spiritual growth. No matter how holy we try to be, we are still imperfect human beings and can be triggered even by Sangha. What we can do is to make sure that we are always conscientious of our own neuroses and learn how to dance around them.

Mundane society does not encourage us to become enlightened; it usually encourages us to pursue conventional goals of success and be ambitious. It does not usually encourage us to become spiritual and seek a transcendent purpose in life or teach us to be compassionate and altruistic. Instead, there is much selfishness and greed. It would be difficult for someone to have a meaningful spiritual path if we were completely immersed in the mundane world with no connection with spiritual community. This is not to say that we have to belong to a Sangha in order to have an authentic spiritual path. As the whole world becomes more secular, human consciousness is also changing. Perhaps there are new models that can help us evolve. Many of the old models are dying. Even though the Sangha is supposed to be a noble community, do not be under the impression that it always is. There are times when it can actually seem to be the wrong community, creating obstacles to awakening rather than supporting it. This depends on who the individuals are who make up the Sangha and also on how you relate to them.

THE UNCONDITIONED REFUGE

Within Chöd practice, we take refuge in the mandala of awakened masters as a source of inspiration and guidance and in the path and wisdom of Chöd as a means of liberation. Being a Vajrayana tradition, there are further levels of refuge that are more advanced: the outer, inner, secret, and ultimate levels. These get more profound as each progressive level of refuge is taken. There are two ways to take refuge: one with form and one without form. Taking refuge in lineage masters, such as Jigme Lingpa and Shakyamuni Buddha, is the refuge of form, because these historical figures are in our minds and hearts. They are not metaphysical or mythological entities; they lived in a particular time in history. Taking refuge can also be done without form, which means to not have an image in our minds. We can have a profound sense of taking refuge by simply opening into ultimate understanding, by intuitively connecting to the sacred within. All forms, no matter how sacred, are not the ultimate refuge. Ultimate refuge is indescribable, unconditioned. Mind has a hard time grasping this because it goes beyond the usual idea of refuge as someone who is going to save us.

In Mahayana and tantric teachings, the Buddha also refers to the Dharmakaya Buddha, or formless Buddha, which is not a person or supernatural being but rather the unconditioned true nature of each of us that is already perfect. When we take refuge, though, it is often easier for most people to have an image—a form—for this formlessness to help our minds connect to it. In the path of Chöd, we take refuge while visualizing the sacred configuration of a mandala, vividly brought to mind through visualization. Sacred iconography such as *tangkas* or statues can be useful supports for generating clear mental images. Visualizing in this way can powerfully invoke the experience of taking refuge in something greater than the illusions and life conditions that we cling to.

In the *Uttaratantra*, a text revealed by the fourth-century Indian master Asanga, the ultimate refuge is stated to be only the Buddha. This does not mean the external Buddha but rather the enlightened nature in each of us. The ultimate Buddha has no form. In this sense, even the sacred visualizations and illustrations of enlightened beings, like Vajradhara, are merely pointing out the inner essence of ultimate refuge. In the *Diamond Sutra*, the Buddha stated,

"Someone who looks for me in form or seeks me in sound
is on a mistaken path
and cannot see the Tathagata."

One cannot find the ineffable Dharmakaya Buddha in any conditioned form. It is not an expression of a theistic or omnipresent phenomenon. It is pointing to our true original nature, which transcends all of our limiting egoic identities.

In *The Dakini's Laughter*, the central figure, Vajradhara—the dark blue image of the primordial buddha—expresses the quintessence of buddhahood itself, beyond all forms and limitations. He appears wearing a crown, adorned with elaborate attire and ornaments, sitting in the cross-legged lotus-seat posture, holding bell and vajra, and is surrounded by various tantric deities. Above Vajradhara is a pyramid of lineage masters, visualized as a source of inspiration: Samantabhadra, Padmasambhava, Yeshe Tsogyal, Machig Labdrön, Longchenpa, and Jigme Lingpa. Machig Labdrön's name is not mentioned in *The Dakini's Laughter*, but it is important to visualize her in this assembly. By taking refuge in this visualized field, our consciousness is pulled away from the vortex of habits. The mundane consciousness is redirected to join the enlightened consciousness of love, joy, awareness, and transcendence. The pure awareness suddenly aligns with the sublime mind, the mind that transcends ordinary thinking mind. This redirects the consciousness into a fearless state—egoless and full of love—releasing our usual tendencies to contract.

Though we visualize Vajradhara, we are not taking refuge in a male supernatural being. In the Tibetan language, gender pronouns are not used as often as they are in many Western languages. We can write or have a long conversation about someone and their characteristics without constantly using gender pronouns to describe them. Western language is extremely logical and detailed and is only made clear to the listener by using gender pronouns. It gets tricky for Westerners to speak about tantric deities because of this use of gender pronouns. For example, Vajradhara appears in the form of a male, but the moment you call him "he" or "him" Vajradhara becomes anthropomorphized. This is a total misunderstanding of the real nature of the sacred image. As *The Dakini's Laughter* states, we are ultimately taking refuge in *rigpa*, the Buddha mind, which is the awakened state of consciousness of ourselves and of those deities. This is why a powerful, energetic shift can take place while taking refuge: our consciousnesses are pulled away from mental habits and redirected to inner love, compassion, awareness, and transcendence. This happens right away: we suddenly no longer feel in alignment with ego but with this sublime mind.

In addition to the different levels of consciousness mapped out in Buddhist psychology, there is a sublime state of consciousness in our imaginations. The question is: How do we imagine this state? We imagine this as a wholesome state full of love, not as our default state of mind, controlled by ego. Meditators and spiritual practitioners might imagine this state as egoless and without ordinary limitations. I have met people in my life who have told me of their nondual experience of awakening. I trust the validity of their claims. Such experiences might happen often or may have happened only once in the past, but they serve as reference points to a state of mind that is above everyday-life consciousness. They can take refuge in this state of mind, whether they are experiencing it in the moment or not. Or if someone has not had a glimpse of nondual awakening, they may have a conceptual understanding of it and can take refuge in that understanding. Simply taking refuge in the sublime state of consciousness lets us lose the unconscious hook into ego mind and begin to ascend to a higher state of consciousness, whatever it is called, rigpa, the buddha mind, or pure awareness.

8

Bodhicitta

In order to cut through
the mind that grasps appearances as real
and to realize the true nature of all things,
I give rise to bodhicitta without hope and fear.

—*The Dakini's Laughter*

Most of the practices in tantric Buddhism begin with taking refuge and then move on to developing bodhicitta. These are the two essential foundations upon which each Tibetan practice rests. Though the nature of bodhicitta does not change with context, the methods for arousing it in the practitioner are unique to each tradition. Developing bodhicitta is a fulcrum of the Chöd sadhana and is included in every Chöd liturgy. According to the classical treatises, bodhicitta is the aspiration to awaken all beings, including ourselves, by treading the path of loving-kindness, compassion, joy, and equanimity, and by practicing the six perfections, or *paramitas*: generosity, discipline, tolerance, diligence, meditation, and wisdom. Within the outlook of Chöd, as *The Dakini's*

Laughter shows, bodhicitta is understood in the context of reification: that we make something out of nothing and then become attached to our concocted version of reality. We become bound inside by dualistic mind manufacturing notions of good and bad, beautiful and ugly, perfect and imperfect, likeable and unlikeable. Bodhicitta is to cut through this dualistic mind by dropping hope and fear right now on the spot, in order to awaken all beings, to help others find the highest liberation in themselves.

Developing bodhicitta is giving rise to the most noble aspiration that a human being can hold. It is not like wishing for more money, success, or worldly glory, but rather it aims for something extramundane such as nirvana, enlightenment, or absolute freedom. The commitment is to use any means necessary to actualize such a vision, not only for personal benefit but for the sake of all beings. Such a state of mind may seem unnatural to us because humans are typically self-centered and act only for our own benefit. This may be true to a certain extent, but there is also a greatness in the human spirit. Sometimes people do act selflessly and courageously on behalf of others, which can be shocking to witness. The altruistic concern for others is in us and often guides our actions in large and small ways, without any need to make news headlines of our heroic acts. If such a motivation were not an innate part of humans, not part of our DNA, then perhaps no one would be talking about this topic at all. Developing bodhicitta is in fact natural to us. It becomes an obvious truth once we intentionally practice it.

Developing bodhicitta has to involve authentic love and compassion. Otherwise, the whole process becomes a grand, lofty, and insincere endeavor lacking any power to change our consciousness. The boundless qualities of love, compassion, empathetic joy, and equanimity are referred to as the four immeasurables. They are "immeasurable" because with each of them we hold an immeasurable number of beings in our hearts. Immeasurable love is the aspiration that all beings without exclusion be happy. Compassion is the aspiration that all beings be free from suffering. Empathetic joy is the wish for all beings to have and never lose happiness. Equanimity is a state of mind free from bias, hatred, and preference in relation to all beings. Sometimes the order of these changes. Some masters might put equanimity first, while others put compassion before love. The order works differently for different individuals. For some people compassion is easier to develop than love. Once they feel compassion, love follows naturally. It is powerful to practice the four immeasurables while visualizing a field of beings—family members, parents, friends, enemies, all of humanity, all living beings. Once your heart is completely open to all of them, you let go of bias, anger, judgement, hatred, and aversion. A space opens in your consciousness in which you can develop true bodhicitta.

Bodhicitta has two aspects in the traditional texts: the bodhicitta of aspiration and the bodhicitta of engagement. The bodhicitta of aspiration is our desire to wake up in order to bring all beings to the highest freedom. Bodhicitta of engagement is more than just having a noble aspiration, a noble wish for others. It means having a sincere commitment to practice the means of awakening, such as the six paramitas, in order to bring about the highest liberation to all beings. It is the commitment to walk the talk. Someone who holds this aspiration is called a *bodhisattva*. A bodhisattva must both aspire for and engage in activities to help others. This includes all activities: from alleviating the smallest pain to helping other beings find unconditional freedom. Some texts use the phrase "embracing samsara," meaning to hold tender awareness for and work tirelessly to alleviate the suffering of beings, the terrible forces binding them to confusion, and their tendency to perpetuate misery. This is the challenge of the bodhisattva.

It is important here to understand that developing bodhicitta is not merely a grand ideal for taking beings to some extraordinary enlightenment. It can be translated into precise and definitive activity, engaging with the world to help people in a very concrete way, such as feeding the hungry. It may be on large scale, such as saving lives during a disaster, or as Shantideva said in his well-known text, *The Way of the Bodhisattva*, as simple as looking at others with honesty and loving-kindness. This could be as simple as smiling at strangers. Though smiling is not a heroic act that deserves a gold medal or the Noble Peace Prize, it is a simple action that can be part of an authentic aspiration to help others all the time. The point is not so much that we need to smile constantly when we encounter someone, which can become insincere and pretentious, but rather it means to genuinely practice loving-kindness as much as possible for everyone without exception.

In *The Way of the Bodhisattva*, Shantideva says,

May I become a protector for those who are helpless.
May I become a guide for those who are traveling.
For those who want to cross the water,
may I become a boat, ship, and bridge.

All the realms of sentient beings
reaching as far as the limits of the sky,
until they all go beyond sorrow,
may I become the source of benefit to them.

These verses express both the heroic aspects—willingness to go to any length to be of service—and the more ordinary engaged methods for expressing loving-kindness. It is not a statement of some profound philosophical theme, yet it helps to understand the comprehensive scope of bodhicitta. Without engaging with the world, bodhicitta becomes an abstract notion, a lofty idea that does not motivate us to take action to help others in real situations. It is possible for higher ideals to become intoxicating and, when they remain just ideals, to produce no direct or beneficial actions on behalf of others. Bodhicitta can be turned into a notion of spiritual sentimentality, which can lead to false transcendence, spiritual bypassing, and lack of real engagement with the world. It can become another of ego's entertainments.

My high regard for some Buddhist teachers comes not just because they are famous or because they are part of a renowned institution. I hold many teachers in the highest esteem, with deep gratitude in my heart for their wisdom. But it is not their fame or position that moves me to see them as bodhisattvas. Once I saw a photo of a lama helping nomads move their truck out of the mud. He seemed unafraid to get dirty and work hard to help others. Regardless of his high status, he stood in the mud with his shoulder pressed into the back of the truck helping to push it. It is unusual for someone in his position to lend a hand like this. But seeing him standing in the mud, I could see who he genuinely was inside. He was not just taking advantage of a photo opportunity, but he wholeheartedly stepped into a real situation, just like that, and offered his help. Our integrity manifests through these simple gestures, rather than through big performances or public commendations. Kind gestures in everyday life really show who we are.

Engaged bodhicitta practice includes becoming aware of our thoughts and feelings toward others as well, not just to the practice of benevolent actions. If such self-reflection is not done, our hearts will be devoid of compassion and we may be unkind toward others. Self-reflection can help bring unkindness to the surface and reveal that we might be judging others harshly. Judging others is a form of being unkind even if it only happens in our minds. It is often difficult to recognize negative thinking about others because it becomes habitual. Therefore, it is important to check our minds and question whether we feel hatred or judgement toward anyone. Putting anyone down because of their social status, religion, race, gender, or history is harmful to others and to ourselves. So, we must ask ourselves: "Do I judge others? Do I hate them? Do I put any of them down?" If so, we have room to develop more bodhicitta. We have more homework to do. Hatred and judgement are habits that are difficult to turn around, partly because we tend to deny or overlook that we harbor such thoughts. Most often, we think it is someone else's problem. The greatest hindrance to bodhicitta is not lack of knowledge about what bodhicitta is. Rather, it is when we think we know all about it and become intoxicated with the ideal while not showing real love and compassion to others. This is what highjacks bodhicitta.

There is a story about the Tibetan monk Patrul Rinpoche in which he wanders somewhere in Tibet and comes across a monk in a meditation cave. Patrul Rinpoche asked him how long he had been in retreat. The monk replied that it had been so many years that he had lost track. Patrul Rinpoche was impressed and asked him, "What has your main practice been all these years?" The monk said, "Patience." But Patrul Rinpoche mischievously pretended he did not hear the monk's answer and asked again, "What did you say?" So, the monk answered more loudly, "Patience." Patrul Rinpoche pretended several times that he did not hear and kept repeating the question, receiving the same answer louder and louder each time. Finally, the monk got irritated and shouted, "I've told you many times, my practice has been patience! Are you deaf?!" Then Patrul Rinpoche said, "The patience you've been practicing must be an interesting version of patience!" Of course, in this way Patrul Rinpoche was able to teach the monk that he had more homework to do. This anecdote illustrates what a powerful obstacle it can be to intellectualize bodhicitta or cherish a thought of having achieved something. All spiritual people should be careful of this. It happens at all levels of practice.

Bodhicitta practice reveals human experience free from egoic reference. By contrast, most of our everyday life experience centers around ego, the sense of me and mine. We have occasional spontaneous openings into spacious mind that are not contracted by ego reference, such as, "I like this or that," "This should not be happening to me," "He or she is dangerous," or "I'm better or worse than others." Even though the occasional moments of freedom between these thoughts are not really bodhicitta, ego reference does subside for a moment and becomes less pivotal. These moments are not necessarily a spiritual experience but are akin to being "in the zone," or having a peak experience. They can be labeled "spiritual" or not, which is up to the interpreter. True bodhicitta, however, is more than just this periodic break. It comes with profound insight and complete freedom from egoic contraction.

In the context of Chöd, developing bodhicitta is the vow to practice the radical path to cut through the root of delusion, hope, and fear in this very lifetime, on this very spot. Hope and fear are the basis of almost all human misery, and being free of hope and fear is the realization of bodhicitta. That is why the Buddhist masters synthesized the whole sense of human suffering with the aphorism, "All beings suffer from not getting what they want and getting what they do not want." Though it sounds simple, it turns out to be the basis of the psychology of suffering. We are all suffering because of not getting what we want or from getting what we do not want—not getting the things we fantasize about and getting the things we have resistance to. The spell of hope and fear obscures our consciousness, keeping us mesmerized by ego's deception.

Stepping onto the bodhisattva path is to commit to bring bodhicitta into our consciousness. This begins by taking the bodhisattva vow, granted by a Dharma teacher or through a sacred vow to your-self. Establishing bodhicitta means to hold it firmly in your heart. It is more than simply reciting a liturgy, which may only give a fleeting feeling of it. Developing bodhicitta is about training our minds and hearts to continually hold it in the deepest place of our being, so that it becomes part of who we are rather than a temporary experience. We need a sense of urgency—that enough is enough. Seeing the pointlessness of continual suffering, we see that there is no time to fool around, no time to squander.

Even though hope and fear are natural human responses to life's circumstances, in some ways the modern world exacerbates them more than ever. Spellbound by a value system based on materialism and meritocracy, people are dissociated from a basic sense of goodness, from their bodhicitta mind. Each age seems to have this same fundamental challenge of hope and fear, but these days not only do we desire material objects but objects of desire are endless. There is just *so much*, and everything is made more extreme by marketing. We are more subject to the swing of hope and fear than ever before.

Exhaustion with samsara is a strong motivation for the instinct to look inward and radically transform. This life on earth can be painful; it is not a paradise. At the same time, even though we are not able to avoid hardships and difficulties, there is a way that we do not have to habitually suffer so much. One of the main roots of our suffering does not lie in external conditions but a state of mind within each of us. We are almost addicted to suffering without knowing it. As the Russian novelist Dostoyevsky said, "Man is sometimes extraordinarily passionately in love with suffering." He is right on this point. We have to fundamentally change our attitudes toward life and make a radical paradigm shift in order to become just as passionately in love with the freedom of an open heart as we are with the one captured in perpetual suffering. It is not to say that we should not suffer but that we can move past the addiction to suffering. It is clear that suffering has no end if we indulge it.

Someone can suffer all the time and never really have the insight or ability to feel exhausted from their painful patterns. It is a common truth that people who continually suffer often do not know why they are suffering or how to step away from it. The suffering becomes a vicious circle and continues to run their lives. An unfortunate human tendency is that people usually do not suffer alone. When we suffer, we tend to inflict pain on others. As the saying goes, "Misery loves company." We tend to impose our misery on others through hatred, judgement, and projection. It is easy to rationalize such behavior through unawareness. We do not see it as purely our own state of mind. Our ego is always playing devil's advocate, rationalizing why we should be unhappy and tormented inside.

Babies experience pain and pleasure mainly from sensory stimulation. They do not have a complex ego structure or the ability to concoct stories and rationalize them. They live every moment with pure experience. They cry when hungry and are soothed when fed. When held warmly, they fall asleep. As we grow, our senses of happiness and suffering become much more complex. We begin to construct a dualistic paradigm that sees the people we deal with, the places we are, our mountains of possessions, and life circumstances as the causes of sorrow and happiness. But by turning inward, we develop discernment and wisdom about this and begin to recognize that suffering and happiness can be a state of our own minds.

This is not to say that all our of experiences are pure illusion. Pain is part of life. Life begins with the physical pain of birth. As we grow older and lose innocence, suffering becomes more psychological. The difference between pain and suffering cannot be told to a small child. But for more mature people, this ability to distinguish is a form of transcendence. A friend told me that he did a long *vipassana* retreat in an orthodox, strict form. Some regard this type of retreat as Buddhist boot camp training. His routine was getting up early in the morning and sitting all day in the same meditation posture with little food. Because he had not sat in that posture for so long before the retreat, he had physical pain. In his mind, he felt like his knees were breaking. He was tormented and angry inside. He entertained thoughts of running away from the whole thing. But part of him said, "Just continue for a while!" Then he had a profound breakthrough. He experienced the difference between pain and suffering. This deep realization was not just a lofty idea. It felt to him like big wisdom that he was able to apply to his life. It was a turning point for his relationship with himself. He realized that pain is pain and cannot be denied and that suffering comes from the resistance to pain. He stopped reacting to the pain so much and was able to sit with it, becoming more benevolent to it. Suffering frequently comes from the story lines that ego constructs around pain. Ego intensifies the degree of the pain in our minds by resisting it. This adds to the pain and suffering by concocting a feeling that life is not fair. This kind of insight about the demarcation between pain and suffering can be a powerful demonstration that suffering is a state of mind.

Understanding the difference between pain and suffering is profound. It is a form of enlightenment. When people practice meditation, this truth develops as a realization. The immediate effect and benefit of staying present in awareness—while going through physical discomfort or through life's difficulties—reduces huge amounts of suffering. It is very simple and has a very profound effect on life. This recognition is part of the bodhisattva's path, which teaches that the path is based on compassion and wisdom. Wisdom does not have to be flashy or a big epiphany. It can be as simple as this recognition of the difference between suffering and pain.

There are countless examples of how pain becomes suffering in everyday life. For example, you may have forgotten to eat lunch and you are hungry. This is a form of pain. It is easy to construct lots of story lines about hunger, thinking "I don't like this feeling" or blaming it on someone who forgot to cook for you. It can develop into a feeling of being ignored or insulted. We can start resisting the feeling of hunger, and the more we resist, the more painful it becomes. Our ego drags us into endless narratives: "My wife or husband forgot to bring me food!" "I never get enough to eat!" Becoming exhausted from suffering is not a matter of transcending human biology— injury, grief from loss, and emotional challenges still occur as part of the flow of life. But we can develop the wisdom to not spin out on these events, to feel the immediacy of the painful situation and not cultivate further suffering by generating elaborate stories.

One time I heard a story that Khenpo Jigme Phuntsok lost his sister, who had been extremely kind to him. Khenpo Jigme Phuntsok is one of the most well-known Tibetan masters in our time. He was like a dignified mountain, always in a state of equanimity, and a kind presence. But when his sister died, he was quite sad. He was grieving. One of his disciples asked, "You are such an enlightened person, please do not grieve." They wanted to console him, but they misunderstood enlightenment as a state where we do not feel human emotions. Khenpo Jigme Phuntsok said, "You don't understand the Dharma. It is not about *not* having a human experience. You must correct that impression." Enlightenment is not about transcending human emotions. It is about seeing that suffering is just a state of mind, driven by ego, habits, attachment, and our tendency to get lost in the mental proliferation of story lines. Once this crucial awakening happens, we can clearly see the possibility of ending suffering.

Some of our suffering comes from our relationships to the external world and people. Because we are social creatures, our relationship to others is the very thing that allows us to survive. But we traumatize each other due to lack of awareness, which is why sometimes people want to run away from the world. We can never be completely isolated—we could not find food or clothing without others. We cannot create the world from scratch. But there are also times that the human world feels like a battleground. Some people tend to view it as a survival game, always trying to win affection, love, and approval, so that the world will proclaim how good, beautiful, and strong we are. The urge to pursue such acclaim causes greed and prevents us from feeling compassion and empathy with fellow human beings. This is the essential trap of what Buddhism calls the eight worldly concerns. The eight worldly preoccupations are what govern our actions: hope for happiness and fear of suffering, hope for fame and fear of insignificance, hope for praise and fear of blame, and hope for gain and fear of loss. These eight worldly concerns are classifications of attachment and aversion that bind us to suffering. We cycle through them until we are released from them into the state of enlightenment.

First, we hope to be happy and fear suffering. When we feel happiness, we are afraid to lose it. When suffering arises, no amount of dreaming makes it go away. Our struggle to make things other than they are only increases our pain. Often people are caught up in internal conflict, wanting to be happy—whatever that means to each individual—while being afraid of what is perceived as unfavorable conditions. This conflict is ongoing in our minds until we are able to cut through the underlying hope and fear.

Second, we hope for fame and fear insignificance. The smallest compliment can stimulate ego's wish for esteem. The mildest gesture or expression can make ego fear denigration or being unpopular. Ego constantly chases after a favorable position in the eyes of the world, continually falling short. Imagined slights only magnify the fear of being insignificant.

Third, we hope to be praised and fear blame. Not only do we crave being recognized by the world, but we also grasp after acclaim. We hope the world will continually proclaim us as being the best. In the meantime, we frantically cover our mistakes out of fear of being caught out as the one who made them and blamed for the world's collapse.

Fourth, we hope for gain and fear loss. The roller coaster of gain and loss is continual. Awards, more money, affection, lots of friends, a bigger house, a better car—we desire every luxury, every material or spiritual reward. Yet with gain, there is loss. Material possessions break down, fade, degenerate. The value of money and goods fluctuates with global conditions. We anxiously seek to freeze our material and spiritual assets at the height of their value, so we never have to experience loss. This feeds an underlying anxiety that is never soothed.

All of the eight worldly concerns have to do fundamentally with the desire for physical pleasure, as well as feeding ego's self view. Human beings are bound by the eight worldly concerns, as if by invisible chains we are not aware of. We become an unending source of not just personal suffering but of interpersonal conflicts and global wars. The eight worldly concerns are about more than just survival—they become convolutions of neurotic patterns, trapping us in endless cycles of misery.

Leo Tolstoy illustrates the trap of the hope for gain in his short story, "How Much Land Does a Man Need?" In the story, a farmer strikes a deal to buy some land. For a sum of one thousand rubles, he can walk around as large an area as he wants, starting at daybreak, claiming all he traverses before returning to his starting point by sunset. If he fails to return before the sun sets, he will forfeit his money. But if he makes a full circuit, he will own all that he has stepped foot on during the day. In his desperate need for more, he decides to run so that he can cover more ground. Exhausted at day's end, he returns to his starting point just before sunset. Unfortunately, having strained himself to the limit, he immediately dies of a heart attack. The story points out that greed becomes neurotic when we try to gain more than we need to survive. Even though many things we do in life are simple survival techniques, survival motivation is easily hijacked by ego.

In modern society, we are told that we can be anybody we want to be. This aspiration tends to inflame narcissism, though. The need for recognition can cause people to behave in cruel and unfortunate ways. Capitalist society tells us we can amass as much fortune as we want. People feel empowered but must compete with everybody else to get the best. The basic impulse to survive becomes egotistic because it would do anything in order for *me* to survive. There is a simple urge to survive in the natural world. Cows, dogs, turkeys, monkeys, and even squirrels will do their best to survive. The human race, however, gets egoistically hijacked in our urge to survive. Humans tend to suffer mentally and psychologically and to fall into a biological spell. The sense of struggle and reward is mesmerizing to the ego.

On the path of Chöd, we are able to see the whole game of ego. The spell is broken and we cut through, severing all worldly concerns, including greed and attachment to approval. We drop them all on the spot. There are stories of Chöd yogis who intentionally do things that seem counterintuitive. They intentionally destroy what we would normally want to protect. They may throw away wealth or do unconventional things that do not promote their image. Some may have walked away from great glory, a high position, great gain, or great wealth. They just walk away.

Modern Chöd practitioners may also act unconventionally like this, though it appears differently with our current cultural norms. For example, a friend of mine helped start a successful software company many years ago. Being one of the founders of the company, she received many stock shares that became quite valuable, worth several million dollars. But the whole time, she felt her life force being drained by technology. She felt that her sense of humanity and authenticity were lost. Though she would have made millions by staying until the stock options matured, she quit the job. Her friends and family thought she was crazy, but not living her truth far outweighed the promise of monetary gain. This was her step into the unknown, cutting the conventions of greed and ambition. This is one small, modern form of cutting the root of attachment to the eight worldly concerns. It is a radical method and goes against every kind of impulse that self-centered ego stands for. Such a path should be a lifelong practice, because one moment of letting go of attachment to something is soon followed by another attachment that can entrap us again.

Developing bodhicitta in the context of Chöd is about having the commitment to take on a radical path from now on, to continually free ourselves in order to help others. Chöd practitioners go to places that invoke fear or anxiety. They intentionally invite fear so that they can cut through it. The radical way means that you do something that brings you to the powerful edge, where you meet with your inner demons or darkness. You invite your fear or desire—you put yourself into situations of wanting approval, recognition, or fortune—so that you can sever or transcend it right there on the spot. You cut through it with radical action. You walk away from fortunes intentionally or just go face to face with the inner demon without getting caught up in it. You just drop it right there on the spot.

Bodhicitta in this context is the vow to practice this radical path in your life from this moment on. You vow to wake yourself up from the prison of ego, delusions, and old concepts, to free yourself from the eight worldly concerns, and to wake others up to the same liberation.

9

Mandala

I arrange this illusory form, my cherished body,
as heaps of a mandala,
and I offer it freely to the field of enlightened deities.
May I cut through the root of self-grasping.
                              —*The Dakini's Laughter*

Mandala practice involves offering the entire universe, including all the riches of existence and sense pleasures, to the sacred. The traditional tantric ritual activity for mandala offering is to arrange beautiful objects and precious gems together, making piles of them on a plate, representing the cosmos. The special plate is held in the practitioner's lap, and heaps of the treasure mixture are poured into each different direction. In the Nyingma tradition, as each recitation of the verse is completed, the plate is swept clean, and then offerings are made again with the next recitation, until all one hundred thousand recitations are complete. Though the beautiful objects and gems being offered are tangible, the more significant offerings are whatever bliss, merit, and inspiration are being held in the heart and mind of the practitioner. These are the nonmaterial offerings of mind, encompassing all precious material and immaterial substances.

We can see the power of giving even in mundane ways throughout many cultures. We often express our love and reverence through offering something tangible to express our love and reverence. And, as we do in a ritual, we frequently invite the others to witness and celebrate these offerings, like for birthdays. Or we may give money to help someone overcome their struggles. Giving a gift makes the giver feel a sense of joy from being generous. We can understand this in the neurological sense—that it releases "feel-good" chemicals—or in a more elevated, spiritual sense that the feeling of letting go when we practice generosity is joyful. Rituals for expressing love are not just important in our conduct within earthly relations but also in our relationships with the sacred. Making offerings to the sacred is a universal way to show reverence for that which is greater than our mundane human existence.

Offering often has a celebratory association; it opens our hearts and is inspiring. Unlike giving money to the government or a tax collector, making heartfelt offerings to the divine brings joy. We could say "I'm offering," or we could say "I *must* give." The first feels good, whereas the second is more challenging. If you are told to give something away and you will not have anything left, it does not feel good. Even though we know it is the same thing in the end, it has a different effect on our minds. Offering is a pure letting go and represents the deep reverence and devotion of the practitioner and their ongoing connection to the divine.

In some cultures, people believe that deities call the shots for humans, determining their fate and the patterns of the phenomenal world. Offering to gods and spirits is a means to please them and stay in their favor. Making offerings is also a big part of Eastern spiritual culture, including Buddhism. This is called *puja* in Sanskrit, meaning "reverence," "honor," and "worship." A puja ritual ceremony often includes offering light, flowers, and water or food to the divine. People tend to be ecstatic when they make offerings, with a feeling that they are connecting to the divine and getting out of a constricting sense of self. Similarly, in some Buddhist cultures, lay people make offerings of food to monastics during their alms rounds. Sometimes Buddhist practitioners will give huge donations to religious projects like building a temple. Both giver and receiver experience joy in that moment of exchange, regardless of the amount of the offering.

Though these practices have been done for centuries, most lay Buddhists do not understand their transcendent basis. To the lay Buddhist practitioner, making offerings of precious substances is simply an expression of love and a cultural ritual. However, in tantric Buddhism offering a mandala is crucial and has to do with more than just showing our reverence to the sacred. Among its many purposes, mandala offering is principally a profound philosophy of letting go of ego and transcending attachment. It is more than just pleasing the deities and buddhas. Even though the buddhas and bodhisattvas and lineage gurus of a mandala are visualized in our minds and we are offering to them, the offering is not *for* them. They are not like a shamanic or Greek god who can be bribed into giving us what we want in response to the offering. Rather, the whole process is a method for transforming the practitioner's consciousness. Who is sacred, anyway? The sacred is just a reflection of our own buddha nature.

Another reason that offering practices in Buddhism are so joyful is that they are connected to the two accumulations, *sambhara* in Sanskrit and *tsok* in Tibetan. These are the accumulation of wisdom and the accumulation of merit. Generally, the accumulation of wisdom comes about from spiritual practices such as self-inquiry, meditation, reflection, awareness, and insight into no-self and emptiness. The accumulation of merit include spiritual practices that are done verbally and physically, like mantra recitation, generosity practices, and altruistic actions on behalf of others. This is not like counting brownie points or hoarding money. Though we cannot measure it with precise numbers, the traditional concept of these accumulations is that the more we practice good deeds such as acts of generosity and meditation, the more joy, love, and wisdom increases in our consciousness. This is a fact that we all can witness, both in ourselves other practitioners. In one sense, the notion of accumulation psychologically encourages us to continue practicing by giving us the conviction that Dharma and virtue can be cultivated in our consciousness to the same degree as we can cultivate anything in the physical world.

People tend to be very involved in possessing money, comfort, and belongings, which can lead to understanding this accumulation as the same. But our attitude toward the accumulations must be clearly understood, or else it becomes a simple materialistic view. The risk is that we only further enhance our pride and ego if we do not clearly hold the true understanding and attitude while making offerings. Some Buddhists act as though there is an invisible bank somewhere in the universe and they can keep putting money into it every time they do something good in their minds. This leads to situations where people are not coming from the right attitude or a true understanding of the accumulations. Some perform virtuous deeds with the wrong motivation or by mechanically going through the motions, believing they are getting a ticket to nirvana. They continually build many stupas or give money to temples. But lacking the right intention of true generosity and love and the sincere aspiration to change their consciousness, their offerings become something they are doing just for themselves. True generosity is boundless and unquantifiable. Therefore, the real meaning behind the two accumulations is to engage in offering activities and actions with the right attitude: the sincere aspiration to change our states of consciousness and be of benefit in the world.

If someone decided to accumulate merit through generosity, they could engage in a concrete way by saying, "Today I am going to donate this amount of money to this charity, next week I will not go out to dinner but will use the money to feed the homeless, and later I will offer money to a legal defense fund." In this sense, it is not just a great deed performed one time but is a commitment to practice generosity all the time. These accumulations are not determined by what you do but by the motivation behind it. All the virtuous deeds without the right motivation would not accumulate merit and wisdom and would not have the power to transform our consciousness.

———

To truly understand the vastness of the mandala ritual, we must hold Buddhist cosmology in minds. In Buddhism, we call the entire galaxy "the three-thousand-fold universe." At the center of the universe is an enormous mountain called Mount Meru, which is surrounded by vast oceans. In the four directions are four great continents: Purvavidheha in the east, Jambudvipa in the south, Godaniya in the west, and Uttarakuru in the north. These are all surrounded by smaller subcontinents and are endowed with treasures and materials, all the precious substances of the world, and the sun and moon. We imagine offering the world to the field of buddhas, bodhisattvas, lineage holders, gurus, and ishtadevatas. Through this visualized act of giving, the practitioner feels an energetic joy of letting go. The heart and consciousness expand. Instead of holding back, we release the painful energy of wanting to protect the personal self by hoarding riches. The suffering of ego contraction—attachment, fear, and greed—is freed through the act of offering vast, joyful riches.

I have encountered people who have resistance to these practices, because they do not subscribe to Buddhist cosmology. But this misses the point. Many Vajrayana practices should be regarded as methods for transforming our consciousness rather than as rigid doctrines. Doctrine has to do with beliefs that we make a choice to adhere to with a "my way or the highway" kind of attitude. But these methods are not about belief. They are simply methods that can be used to change the state of consciousness. Whenever someone practices the traditional mandala offering ritual, they should not take the descriptions of the world literally. In Buddhism, there are actually many different systems that describe the world—not just one. The world system in the *Kalachakra Tantra* is slightly different than the one described in the literature of the Abhidharma. The ancient Indian Buddhist mathematician and astronomer Aryabhata described the cosmos even differently—in a way that is surprisingly similar to modern science. It does not matter exactly how the world is imagined to be; what matters is the motivation in the mind of the practitioner making the offering.

The ritual practice of mandala offering—in which the practitioner offers the entire cosmos to enlightened beings—is a form of generosity and is one of the main practices of generating the two accumulations. In the context of Vajrayana, though, it is more than just generosity. It requires much more than just doing good deeds to please the spirits. It is a method of letting go and cutting through grasping on to the egoic self. By including both material and mental substances—such as thoughts, ideas, concepts, emotions, beliefs, feelings, and consciousness—we begin to realize that they are all equal in their essence. There is no good or bad, pure or impure, sacred or profane, beautiful or ugly. Everything in nirvana and samsara are of one taste—*ro chik* in Tibetan. They are insepa-rable and have the same flavor of experience.

The notion of one taste is exemplified in the life of Gendun Chöpel, the renowned Tibetan scholar and cultural icon known for being an intellectual rebel. It is said that a famous monk once went to Gendun Chöpel in order to engage in a scholarly debate. When they met, Gendun Chöpel was smoking a cigarette. He grabbed a statue of Tara and dropped his cigarette ashes on it. The monk freaked out to see a sacred statue desecrated in that way and immediately initiated the debate by launching into an argument that the action was blasphemous. Gendun Chöpel responded that the sacred does not have the same ordinary perceptions of pleas-ant and unpleasant that we do, because it is not a separate being outside of us. With this logic, he completely defeated the monk in the debate. Dropping ashes on Tara was the highest mandala offer-ing because it came from his understanding of one taste.

One taste is also central to the unique mandala offering visu-alization that is done in Chöd. The Chöd mandala is based on tra-ditional mandala offering practice, but here the ancient Buddhist cosmology is connected to our own physical bodies. You actually imagine that you are offering your own body, regarding your torso as Mount Meru, your limbs as the four continents, your extremi-ties as the subcontinents, your head as the realm of the devas, your two eyes as the sun and moon, and your inner organs as the wealth of the devas and humans. In your mind, you offer this body to the sacred, the gurus of the lineage and the enlightened deities, such as ishtadevatas, who are an expression of our awakened mind.

This is a unique method and different from any other form of mandala practice, though it shares the same principles. The reason we turn our bodies into the mandala offering is that the fulcrum of Chöd practice is to cut through our attachment to the personal self. Our body is one of the main phenomena that identifies who we are. We think we *are* the body. And because of this, we think we are separate from everything else. This mistaken belief says that anything within the body is who you are, everything in your mind is who you are, and everything outside your skin is the world of "other." This is understandable because we interact with the world through our bodies. We feel our own aliveness, all pain and pleasure, in our bodies. Without the body, we would not experience life as we know it. But, if we really inquire, this personal self is fundamentally an illusion—we will not find it. Nothing in existence is true evidence for a personal self, whether identified with the body, or consciousness, or mind. Even the body itself is not as concrete as it appears; it is made of trillions and trillions of atoms. If those are looked into, they are only energy. So underneath this seeming reality of a personal self in the body, there is a more vast reality that may be unsettling to some and not to others—that things are not as real as they appear.

To come to this realization requires profound inquiry, which is why in ancient times people had this extraordinary awakening known as *no-self*. This nondual awakening happens spontaneously in people due to auspicious or powerful circumstances. But other than that, it requires deep inquiry to get there. There is sometimes a curiosity in us as to whether this personal self is a fictitious entity, because it seems to permeate human consciousness. People want to find out what lies beneath this personal self and discern whether it is true. The Buddha himself did not teach the view of no-self right away. He recognized that many people were not ready to hear this truth. He only taught it to his advanced disciples who were ready to hear it. The second-century Indian philosopher Nagarjuna is credited with later developing the tradition of Madhyamaka, further refining the philosophical view that postulates that the self is an illusion. To say there is no self is not the same as saying there is no consciousness—there is obviously consciousness, which has the ability to be aware of itself and the world around it. This view says that when consciousness is aware of itself, it gets lost and starts perceiving itself as a separate "me" as opposed to the "outside world." In that sense, the Buddhist stance on the personal self is in juxtaposition to the Western view of René Descartes, who deduced, "I think, therefore I am." He concluded that there is a personal self because of thoughts, whereas if he had been Nagarjuna, he would have concluded, "I think, therefore there is no self." This personal self is not a thing; it is just a powerful concept in our minds.

Here, offering the body as a mandala is a radical way of cutting through the identification with a self. From that point of view, the mandala offering in Chöd can take us all the way up to dropping ego identity. In the end, regardless of whatever form of mandala offering we are practicing in the Vajrayana, it comes down to the experience of letting go of our attachment to self. The idea of offering, or being generous, sometimes comes to us more readily than the idea of letting go of the self. Though, of course, they amount to the same thing in terms of waking up.

The wisdom of offering and letting go does not always have to be lofty or profound; it can be applied to many areas of our lives. I once spoke to a couple going through a divorce. Both were Vajrayana practitioners and wonderful human beings in their own way. I had a very good connection with them. The woman told me they were fighting over money, and she was quite troubled. She wanted to get her share and realized at some point that she was not getting what she wanted. She perceived that she was the loser and her husband the winner. The woman and I had a series of meetings, and I offered my advice as best as I could. At some point, something cracked in her consciousness. She decided not to hold on to the struggle and not to grieve the loss. Her Vajrayana wisdom kicked in, and she decided that her loss was an offering to him. So, if you feel you have to let go of something precious and it is painful or full of struggle and you say instead that you are "offering" it, there can be a sense of joy. This woman did not want to cause pain or get caught up in anger. She used Vajrayana wisdom to regain her equanimity. After this, she told me that she "offered" everything she lost to her husband. It was inspiring to witness the obvious joy on her face and her big smile. In that moment, she was free of struggle, pain, and conflict.

Even good people like these who have good principles can struggle over mundane matters like money. It is common for people who are afraid, grieving, and in conflict to want to get the lion's share because people need money to survive, especially after the shock of divorce. There can be a lot of fear about not being able to live well and pay all the bills, but it is easy to get caught up in greed and lose sight of our integrity. I am not saying we have to let others walk over us or give everything we have away. The point is that my friend, though she did not get everything she wanted, was able to let go of clinging and turn what she lost into an offering.

In the Chöd mandala, we are letting go of our egos and self-grasping, our attachment to self in our minds and bodies. This allows us to enter into the experience of one taste, that emptiness and form are nondual. We are able to see that phenomena, including our selves, are identical in that they lack inherent existence in the realm of the absolute. This is the essence of the mandala offering. Through this offering, the experience of transcendence of personal self and duality can happen right away. It is a celebration of the most difficult offering—our selves.

10

Guru Yoga

In the uncontaminated space of Dharmakaya,
centered in radiant rainbow light,
the father, knower of the three times, Padmakara
appears in the manner of a heruka performing yogic
   conduct.

—*The Dakini's Laughter*

Guru yoga is a Vajrayana method for dropping our egos and our resistance to waking up. At its core, it is about surrender and devotion. This beautiful surrender happens in which we drop our egos and then allow our hearts to open wide. In a moment, we let go of resistance and open to selfless wisdom. Ego typically fortifies itself against surrender and is irritated by groundlessness. It is very hard to surrender ego, which is trapped in the defenses of its neurotic patterns. Surrender does not require a complex skill or knowledge, but ego is a mighty force of resistance even when we are fueled by zeal and dedication to enlightenment. Many spiritual practitioners make extreme efforts in their dedication to the notion of surrender, such as becoming vegetarian, undertaking long pilgrimages, or memorizing many pages of scripture. But someone can do these difficult tasks and still not be able to surrender the self. In fact, ego mind can come to enjoy such self-recognition of these fantastic, holy activities.

The surrender here is not ordinary surrender. It is divine surrender. The difference is that with ordinary surrender, you surrender *to* someone, which is still a game of ego. In this way, ego pretends to surrender but is actually self-gratifying. This often results in endless dismay—a dualistic relationship that is not honest but is just one ego surrendering to another ego. Divine surrender is the surrender of ego, not to someone else's ego but through a catalyst such as devotional trust in a true guru. In the end, it is not as if we are surrendering to a human person or, in formal guru yoga practice, to the sacred form of Padmasambhava or Machig Labdrön, even though it may look like that from the outside. Rather, we are using the principle of divine love as a catalyst for powerful awakening and rising above ordinary consciousness.

Many traditional Tibetan stories describe relationships between guru and student as being the radical means of awakening, using as examples the relationships between the ancient Tibetan masters of the Mahamudra tradition Tilopa and his disciple Naropa and Marpa and his disciple Milarepa. In reading their stories, it seems that Naropa surrendered himself completely to Tilopa, and Milarepa completely surrendered to Marpa. But Tilopa and Marpa were not easy-going gurus. They challenged their students all the time. We have to bear in mind that both Naropa and Milarepa were very intelligent. Before Naropa ran into Tilopa, he had been a great *pandita*, or scholar, and was a teacher in his own right. He was not someone with a lost soul looking for a personal savior. The same was true of Milarepa, who was already an intelligent and strong practitioner before meeting Marpa. Each of them held sincere motivations and intentions in their hearts, and guru and student understood one another. The gurus wanted to help their students wake up, and the students had sincere intentions to wake up. Both teachers challenged their students again and again. The relationships served as powerful paths for rigorously wearing out ego.

Naropa, Milarepa, and all the great *mahasiddhas*, or tantric masters, went through challenging relationships with their gurus. But those gurus were absolutely enlightened, and their only interest was their students' freedom. At every step of the relationship, the gurus asked for the impossible, causing the students to finally and ultimately surrender their egoic propensity toward self-reference and through that to experience complete awakening. The students' trust, love, and respect made the relationships auspicious and effective.

It is important, however, that modern gurus do not use these ancient stories to just bolster their own ego fortress. Gurus should not mimic these ancient mahasiddhas. They must know the history but not try to mimic them by saying to their students, "I'm going to make you do things that make you humble and challenge your ego." This is not healthy. Some teachers may have transcendent wisdom and love, but few are able to teach this way without their own egos getting involved. And as for the students, even advanced practitioners in modern times can get lost in the habit of wanting to be saved from the outside, and this can be a subtle shadow in our minds. True surrender is crucial to true awakening. Surrender is not a one-shot deal but rather a continual examination of our own propensities and a cultivation of the thirst for awakening.

I once heard a story of a highly respected Nyingma lama who was skillfully challenged by a master. He met a yogi who quickly invited him to drink alcohol, but he did not want to drink it. He felt that his position held him to a high standard in the public eye and that he should follow the precept of abstaining from intoxicants. But on the other hand, he respected the yogi. So, he drank the alcohol and had a profound insight in that moment. By surrendering to the yogi and trusting him, he was able to let go of his identity as an important person, to let go of his pompous importance, which he saw as separate from who he really was. His role had become a golden chain, binding him to his persona and its benefits. Drinking the alcohol helped him let go of his image and led him to glimpsing profound freedom. However, we must know that this only works if the teacher is a completely evolved person who does not want anything from the student and the student is not operating under the type of psychological messiness that leads people to join the wrong groups.

A guru-student relationship must be entered carefully. The ancient tantric scriptures offer important guidelines for the qualifications of a true guru. Because many people mistakenly approach a guru as a savior of souls, the traditional scriptures help the tantric student discern genuine qualifications in their teacher. There is a saying in Tibetan culture that for a genuine and beneficial relationship to occur, the guru and student must examine each other for three years before accepting one another as teacher and student. The formal practice of guru yoga is a practice specifically for those who have entered the Vajrayana path, who have the right temperament and state of consciousness to understand and receive benefit from it. With the right understanding, it is a powerful method that can bring up strong emotions and feelings and serve as a potent door to enlightenment. Outside of the context of the Vajrayana tradition, philosophy, and practices, guru yoga can be easily misunderstood.

The heart of guru yoga is devotion, which can also be called divine love. It is a form of non-egoic love held by practitioners toward the guru, their teacher. Sincere students are those who have made a genuine commitment to vigilant introspection and who have developed inner discipline and humility. The journey they make is continuous. The Vajrayana path requires great diligence, not only in our efforts to maintain practice but also in being continually honest with ourselves. A relationship is formed through the initiation ritual of abhisheka, as well as through higher teachings. The basis of receiving the initiation is the practitioner's authentic commitment to the guru. In this radical shift we enter a non-egoic state, which can be called *Dharmakaya mind*, or pure awareness. The formal practice of guru yoga is appropriate only for those who have a guru in their lives, who have been accepted by that guru as a student to guide them in their Vajrayana practice, who have an affinity with the sacred lineages of the past. But the heart of the practice of devotion and divine love can be helpful for anyone. Through it, the ultimate act of transcending self-orientation and challenging a limited view of achievement in spirituality is integral to many traditions.

The noble inner qualities of a genuine guru are not always evident on first meeting but become evident over time through the process of deeply getting to know them. There have been a few famous gurus whose popularity did not necessarily reflect their realization or merit. The teacher-student relationship is too important, with too many possible mishaps, to rush the process of finding a guru or student. Great discernment and maturity on both sides will have mutually beneficial results. It is said that few gurus embody all awakened attributes, but one of the first qualities a guru must have is authentic compassion. Having compassion makes us sympathetic, considerate, and altruistic and prevents us from exploiting others. Deep wisdom and skillful means can be transmitted by teachers who are accomplished in this way, and great benefit can flow to their students through their compassionate guidance. In this way, gurus need not be perfect, and the relationship need not be perfectly smooth. More significant is that gurus should have the integrity and self-awareness to not use or abuse their students and to never ask them to do self-denigrating things. That would be unhealthy for everyone. They hold their student's well-being and spiritual development as a sacred trust. If the guru's motivation and intention are only for their student's well-being and awakening, then the relationship will have positive results.

I must admit I have been very lucky in this life when it comes to my spiritual mentors. The people I regard as my gurus have turned out to be amazing beings. I do not believe I am speaking just from my projections, as I actually tend to be quite skeptical about these matters. One of my gurus was named Lama Tsurlo, with whom I spent much formal and informal time. He was my calligraphy and tangka painting teacher and gave me many abhishekas, teachings, and advice. He was a lifelong hermit, lived as a renunciate, and was completely grounded in his spiritual practice, like an unshakable mountain, never wavering with uncertainty or hesitation. Being strong and compassionate, he never strayed from the path. Without the usual self-concerns, he completely dedicated his life to awakening. When he died, his only remaining possessions were some texts and bowls, a simple expression of his life dedicated to spiritual, not material, pursuits. Another lama I would call my guru is named Lama Garwang. I knew him from quite an early age and received the most important teachings in the Dzogchen tradition from him, which are known as *ngotrö*, or pointing-out instructions. Through this practice, the disciple can recognize the nature of mind when it is pointed out to them by the guru. He was also a renunciate, and the people around him held him in high regard. He was absolutely compassionate. If such a thing as a perfect human being exists, I would consider him one of them.

The teachers I have most admired were regarded as gurus by many people, yet most of them were not spiritual celebrities. I and many of their other students decided to take them as our guru because we saw their true natures as amazing human beings, as true spiritual masters who developed love and compassion. What they taught me changed my life, but when I inquire into it, I learned as much from just being around them and witnessing their goodness as I did from their teachings and initiations. I learned from their compassion and from feeling their kindness. In this way, devotion increases both from hearing the teachings of a guru and by simply being in their presence. When we have devotional trust and love for someone, something opens in us and we are receptive to them. We learn energetically and our being is saturated. We seem to be viscerally imprinted by their goodness.

Love of a guru can be one of the most meaningful ways that we learn, and this is due to our capacity for receptivity. For example, it is clear that many people who started their spiritual paths with Khenpo Jigme Phuntsok ended up going through life-changing experiences. As many as ten thousand monks and nuns lived in his monastery. Many people witnessed that just as he was loving, compassionate, and noble, his disciples were also loving, compassionate, and noble. As human beings experience love toward another, our hearts and minds tend to energetically resonate. When this happens, we become more receptive to the loved one's wisdom. Our consciousness can become infused with their consciousness. We tend to listen to them, and if they say, "Don't be angry, let go," we tend to do it with no resistance. If your loving guru tells you not to be angry or hang onto hatred, you listen to them and try to do it. It is quite logical in the end. When there is divine love, there is much less resistance than there would be to instructions from a stranger. We may not follow even good advice if it is not from someone who is loved in this way.

In guru yoga, the phenomenon of divine love is visualized by imagining that the guru dissolves into our own being. This allows the practitioners to experience their minds mingling with the open, nonconceptual mind of the guru. With devotion, we are therefore able to perceive this experience as Dharmakaya mind and become free from ego in that moment. The guru is visualized in the form of a deity, which really helps give power to our divine devotion. If we were to visualize the guru in their human form rather than one of these familiar archetypal forms, not only is it difficult to generate this divine love, but we might bring in their human idiosyncrasies that then diminish in our minds the radiant quality of their love and wisdom.

No matter how realized, a living teacher is still human. Visualizing a pure form of guru prevents putting the ordinary human, along with their foibles and humanness, on a pedestal. Not everything that a guru does is transcendent. Focusing on their humanness can be an obstacle to connecting with the inner pure goodness of the guru. We do not deny the reality of their human foibles, but during the visualization, used as a method, we do not want them to block our opening to divine love.

There is a famous renunciate in Tibet, held by many to be an enlightened yogi, for whom I have great reverence. When I met him and spent time with him, my respect for him only grew. He radiated pure love wherever he went. I thought of him as a divine yogi without a human side. But by coming to know his human aspects, I began to appreciate him more completely, not just through an idealized view. Someone told me that this yogi had an exceptionally close attachment to his cousins. It was known that he always took their side whenever they ran into trouble, and he became displeased if anyone criticized them. His strong traditional Tibetan family ties were evident in this way. My reverence for him became more mature when I found this out—it became more authentic with less projections. But, on the other hand, to see the guru only in human form can confuse divine love with ordinary human love and can also be filled with attachment and projections. So, the visualizations done in the formal practice are intentionally made in order to see the teacher in a pure form, as a deity. Then, we can be free from the obscurations of confused human attachment.

Divine love is used in many spiritual traditions as a doorway to ultimate awakening—to nirvana, enlightenment, or the divine. It is very real, very visceral. It has been described as the feeling of being drunk with ecstasy. Some ancient monastics wrote poems of fervent and passionate spiritual love. They were suspected of having secret lovers because their writing was so romantic, and not in the abstract. It sounded like someone actually talking about his or her secret lover, which at times caused little controversies. Yet, these monks and nuns were really devoted and did not have physical love with anyone. They brought their love of the Dharma or the sacred into a state of ecstatic divine love.

One of the hinderances in spirituality is that people can become imbalanced. Both extremes of intellectualization and emotional intoxication can lead to missing the point. Divine love is a good antidote to make sure that our spirituality is not too conceptual, heady, or one-sided. It prevents spirituality with a dry heart—being lost in a mental state, filled with intellectual information and theoretical analysis. Through love, we open and do not get trapped in this heady trip. A dry heart is nothing more than a subtle fortification of ego. And when this happens, we cannot surrender. Divine love melts the resistance of ego.

Yet, ego is one of those things we cannot live with and cannot live without. It should not be turned into a scapegoat for all our misery and misadventures. It has many functions for survival. But ego is a trap that resists the unconditioned and holds onto the separate self, which only leads to suffering. In general, many people live day to day without self-reflection and are not concerned with the whole theme of ego. But when someone becomes spiritual, he or she begins to realize the role ego plays as the root of all misery. It is common for them to then go into ego-bashing and have a desire to get rid of it. But this is still an immature understanding, because we cannot actually get rid of ego. It has a role in our existence. The only thing we can do is learn to not get caught in its trap.

In Dzogchen, it is said that in the beginning there is a primordial ground in which nothing is separate. From that, consciousness becomes aware of itself and then separates self from others. That is how ego comes into being. Eventually, that separation will cause suffering. This is the genesis for human misery. Ego is holding on to everything: the story lines, emotions, and beliefs that keep us separate. Somehow divine love loosens this powerful resistance of ego. It is a catalyst for inner freedom, which is why many of the saints and mystics of the past had the courage to spiritually die into this experience.

Guru yoga is a central part of Chöd practice, and each Chöd liturgy has its own version. It works with the sacred forms of the guru, beyond human characteristics. The visualizations in guru yoga are usually a mandala of lineage masters in their sacred forms, surrounding one who presides over the mandala and is considered the main figure. They are often depicted in precise form with certain postures, with hand implements, mudras, and in specific attire, each of which has a symbolic meaning. Specific lineage masters are visualized in a sacred mandala unique to each particular lineage. For example, in *The Dakini's Laughter* the central figure of the guru yoga mandala is Padmasambhava. In other Chöd liturgies, Machig Labdrön or another deity can be the central figure.

In *The Dakini's Laughter*, Padmasambhava is visualized as a carefree yogi in what is called the fashion of an *avadhuta*, a Sanskrit term used to describe mystics, siddhas, or saints who have reached a high level of spiritual awakening. Similarly, in tantric Buddhist iconography, the Tibetan word *zhigpapo* describes masters who do not resemble traditional Buddhist monks with shaved heads and clean robes. They look like wild people, with their hair in top knots, wearing bone ornaments and not too much clothing. These divine madmen abide in an egoless state of consciousness. They demonstrate that they have no attachment to conventional values through actions that lack any care for prestige, power, or wealth. Many of these masters do not play by conventional rules and ignore the guidelines of the religious establishment. The Indian mahasiddha Saraha was one of the first avadhutas, depicted as a half-naked, wild-looking ascetic. He was an awakened master, but his teachings were radical and departed from orthodox doctrine. He had walked away from a prestigious position as spiritual mentor to an Indian king. As a high caste brahmin, he fell in love with an untouchable woman, which was considered a stigma in his time. He followed two women as his gurus, and they gave him profound instructions that led to his awakening.

When visualized as the central figure in a Chöd mandala, Padmasambhava is seen in this avadhuta form as someone living freely as a wandering ascetic, representing the transcendence of conventions and preoccupations. Portrayed as almost naked, except for a tiger-skin skirt, bone ornaments, and top knot, he holds a damaru in his right hand and a trumpet in his left. He is surrounded by a sea of dakas and dakinis in the sky in front of and above the practitioner. In this part of Chöd practice, we arouse intense devotion to Padmasambhava by regarding him as an embodiment of the love, wisdom, and compassion of all the buddhas.

In my experience teaching Vajrayana in the West, I have found that many people have a hard time feeling divine love for their teachers, yet they have much less resistance to feeling love for Padmasambhava or Machig Labdrön. So sometimes I ask them to take Padmasambhava or Machig Labdrön as their own guru and to feel the devotional love toward them. Even though they have not met them in person, they are in the same lineage. This practice of love is very visceral, not conceptual at all, and requires complete divine love for the guru, such that the ego dies in that moment. It is especially powerful for Chöd practitioners who are trained in the Nyingma tradition, because they have already developed a strong affinity for Padmasambhava through other practices. With deep longing, we pray to the ultimate guru to help wake up to freedom from the snare of ego. We also ask the guru to grant blessings to help cut through all the binding inner poisons, right now on this very spot, especially the poisons of hope and fear. Resistance can melt right there.

The principal objective of guru yoga is to realize what is called the "true guru"—the buddha within, or buddha nature. In other words, it is about eventually turning our attention inward and realizing that the true object of divine love is not external but lies within and is the true nature of who we are. In the end, this is all about coming back to ourselves, realizing that our true nature is everything that we have been seeking. It is everything that is revered. Ego has a hard time figuring this out. But guru yoga is a powerful method using this rich experience of divine love to realize our own true nature, which turns out to be a goal for other Buddhist paths as well. In the broader Mahayana tradition, the notion of *tathagatagarbha,* or buddha nature, means that our true nature is already perfect, already enlightened. Mahayana uses various means like inquiry and purification to wake up to the essential nature within. The use of this heart-based divine love is also a central tantric Buddhist practice.

Vajrayana is a powerful path. It is a challenge to the ego in many ways because our ego tends to have a hard time letting go of self and surrendering. Ultimately, this is not about surrendering to anyone—just ego surrendering by itself. It is the hardest thing for humans to surrender our ego. The goal of guru yoga surrender is nondual surrender, which is why eventually we come to the realization that divine love for the guru is divine love for our true nature. Continuing to be ruled by ego causes a host of suffering created by our neurotic tendencies. The alternative to that—this awakening—can bring about the end of suffering.

Guru yoga can be a difficult path in modern times where individualism and secularism are the dominant systems. Many people misunderstand such practices and therefore do not relate to them. We do not surrender our ego to someone else but to the ineffable. True divine love dissolves our self-reference and opens our hearts. We then lose fear and other forms of neuroses. It is an immediate path that can take us to a high level of spiritual awakening.

I often feel that it would be powerful to introduce guru yoga to more Western meditators, and yet I am also concerned that people will resist it and believe that it goes against their values. I know, though, that people are capable of experiencing divine love—pure love that is not mixed with the poison of concepts and unhealthy projections. I have seen this with my own friends and have witnessed real transformation in them. During a retreat in the magical place of Canyon de Chelly, I was moved to see how open-hearted my friends were while doing the Chöd sadhana. We were practicing *The Dakini's Laughter*—with music, instruments, and the haunting Tibetan melody—under a magnificent tree (that some of us called the *bodhi* tree) next to a giant stupa-like sand formation. Periodically, I would notice how everybody was reacting and was moved by the sea of divine love happening in our grove, among this group of Westerners. I felt that many of them were melting into divine love, their hearts were opening, and they were ready to wake up and let go of their resistance. It seemed they were ready to go to the highest place in their consciousness. Both intellect and heart are needed for this transformation. In this way, the heart's job is to help us remain spacious and joyous and less defensive inside. Guru yoga is a way of letting go into love and inner freedom—it is a powerful path to our own hearts.

11

Feast Practice

This coarse body, the remnant of habitual tendencies,
is fat and juicy.
From within that, pristine awareness separates upward
manifesting as Krodha Kali.
—*The Dakini's Laughter*

The most radical practice in Chöd is the body offering ritual—
lujin in Tibetan. It is a form of sacred feast done as a visualization. The inspiration for its origin likely lies in the Mahayana
sutras, but its purpose is greater than doing something wholesome or noble. It is much bigger than just an act of generosity. It
is a method of inviting in all neuroses in the form of archetypal
demons and feeding them our own body in the spirit of kind and
friendly hospitality. Through that, we release our visceral and
energetic attachment to those demons. In giving away the body,
we bless it as made of sacred ingredients—medicine and ambro-
sia—and offer it not only to the archetypal demons but also to the

buddhas and bodhisattvas. Through that we let go of our suffering and feel a wholesome state of mind. Joy and tranquility arise.

The body offering ritual of lujin is all done in the mind. Typically generosity is associated with physically giving objects in person. But in this more esoteric approach, generosity is done mentally, as an unbounded, imagined action. Ordinary generosity is most familiar and is not esoteric but is as simple as common courtesy. However, some may make a great display of it and carry it out with the sense of pompous philanthropy. But people often act generously without labeling it as such. Various traditions emphasize donating money to a charity or giving money for food and shelter to the homeless. Many spiritual traditions practice this virtue as a core principle, though in fact people constantly practice generosity, even outside of a spiritual context. By helping others, everyone benefits and develops a sense of inner satisfaction. *Dana*, the Sanskrit word for the virtue of generosity, carries with it an implication that the desire to give, to help others, is an innate impulse for us.

In Buddhism, generosity is considered the foundation for all other virtues. A bodhisattva is an archetype of a supreme being who gives away everything, shows the way to transcend grasping onto material possessions, and continually lives through altruistic actions. Bodhisattvas go beyond ordinary generosity, giving up even their own enlightenment for the sake of other beings. The example shown by bodhisattvas encourages us to follow in their footsteps and to practice heroic generosity as they do. Even in this present day there are many living bodhisattvas. Witnessing their generosity not only inspires our admiration but also kindles the inspiration to act as they do and to become a bodhisattva.

Each time we give something with the right altruistic intentions, there is a feeling that we become greater inside. There is a sense of transcendence, of joyfully going beyond this limited self and dropping attachment to it. Generosity can be practiced in many ordinary, simple ways, as well as in grand and courageous acts of giving. Even though we usually imagine stories of the heroic bodhisattva's benevolent deeds, many people are generous in their own nature. To them, it is part of ordinary life, not a religious observance dictated by holy scripture. These people do not consider it a virtue, they just practice it as part of ordinary life. Most of us have met someone like this and have been stirred by their easy and open giving. There are many bodhisattvas walking among us. They are the unsung heroes who bless the world with their kindness and generosity.

Once at a meditation retreat a man shared that he had a kidney disease. Without a new kidney, his own would fail and he would surely die. Another person at the retreat decided on the spot to donate one of her kidneys to him. Many people at the retreat knew and loved this young man, but this person had only just met him. She was not seeking any praise or appreciation, so she donated her kidney while remaining anonymous. She was simply moved to make a radical and charitable donation to this man. After receiving his new kidney and recovering, the man was grateful and longed to thank the woman for her generosity, but he did not know who she was. In fact, her generosity was beyond the bounds of needing to be thanked. This was not a fairy tale but a truly heroic act of generosity.

In Tibetan culture, generosity is highly encouraged, and it is woven into many aspects of life. For example, when someone dies in Tibet their body is chopped up and fed to carnivorous birds. This is known as sky burial. Few cultures in the world practice it today, but historical records show this practice was done in Native American and Zoroastrian cultures too. How this practice began is uncertain, but in Tibetan Buddhist culture it is seen as a practice of generosity, of making an offering of the body. The body is first taken to a cemetery where someone—usually a Chöd practitioner—dissects the body into pieces and then invites vultures to feast on it. It is a demonstration of no-self, that the body is not who we are.

The Chöd ritual of offering the body as a feast is not about rejecting or not loving or caring for the body. By offering the body—by generously letting go of our attachment to it—we are able to set free the notion that the body defines the personal self. This notion is an illusion, a figment of the imagination. It is one of the most difficult illusions to wake up from, to let go of. Indeed, identification with the body is perhaps the most powerful illusion that there is, because our whole sensory and relative experience of the world is filtered through the physical body.

To begin the Chöd feast, we visualize the *avadhuti*, or *kundarma* in Tibetan, which is the central energetic channel in the body. Inside of it is a white circle which is visualized around the heart, representing our consciousness. With a sudden, powerful exclamation of "Phet!" we visualize that the consciousness shoots up through the crown of our heads and the body, separated from consciousness, falls to the ground. The white circle immediately transforms into the deity Krodha Kali, who represents profound liberation. This moment of the experience of liberation in our consciousness becomes manifest as the completely pure form of the deity. An energetic shift in consciousness abruptly occurs in the moment of exclaiming "Phet!" We immediately drop ego identification and enter a state of egoless awareness—a consciousness of pure awareness. We drop ordinary thought and become free from all usual contractions, such as fear. It feels big, like we have already gone beyond everything. It feels like transcendence.

Krodha Kali is a wrathful tantric goddess. She often appears as a dark-blue color, like the sky at night, representing the emptiness that pervades everything. She holds a butcher's knife, or kartika, in one hand, which represents the skillful and determined act of severing ego identity. She holds a skull cup of blood in the other hand, which represents the death of samsara. She is joyfully trampling on the demons who represent the inner poisons. In some versions of this practice, Krodha Kali is visualized with the roaring head of a pig behind her right ear. The pig represents the highest Vajrayana transcendence of all concepts—dirty vs. pure, beautiful vs. unattractive—because in real life pigs are known for consuming everything without bias. So, the pig represents complete nonduality, going beyond all concepts and mental elaborations.

This kind of meditation on the archetypal deities can change our states of mind right away. Each of these deities have a special impact on us. For example, if we feel the world is volatile and feel volatile internally, like we are in conflict with everyone, then meditating on the motherly, gentle, kind, compassionate, and serene deity Tara can soothe that inner volatility and invoke a state of peace. Sometimes we need this to counter a sense of imbalance in our lives. We need to be in touch with soothing and gentle energies to induce a peaceful state. Similarly, Krodha Kali brings about an urgency, power, strength, and wrath to cut through attachment to ego and all neuroses. This deity has a dynamism—a dynamic determination to cut through delusion.

The offering feast is not just a way of practicing generosity but is also a radical way of transcending a sense of personal self. Since our body is one of the main bases of egoic identity, letting go of our attachment to it is a primal way to practice ultimate generosity. Through this, we are challenged to liberate the most deeply embedded sense of self. Through visualizing offering our bodies as a feast to demons, we uncouple our closely held associations with the physical body, its karmic obstructions, distorted self-image, and painful contractions. We do this from the state of the pure consciousness of the enlightened energetic body.

Visualizing Krodha Kali commences the four feasts: white, variegated, red, and black. Each one has a distinct visualization and purpose. The four feasts are conducted at different times of the day to coincide with the different energetic qualities, relationship, and activities of these times. Some perform the white feast in the morning, the variegated at noon, the red in early evening, and the black feast at night. The white feast is said to help cultivate the two accumulations of wisdom and merit, the variegated feast is for purifying karmic debts, the red feast is a powerful means of cutting through self-grasping, and the black feast is for purifying negativity.

The Tibetan word for feast, *gyé*, implies that you are not inviting just one guest but a huge crowd of many kinds of guests to enjoy the feast. Next we invite and visualize buddhas, bodhisattvas, mahasiddhas, and ishtadevatas as revered guests. We also invite all sentient beings from all the realms. We imagine that the whole assembly of guests begin to consume the feast offering and are completely fulfilled by it. The moment all beings consume the feast, they become satisfied, utterly fulfilled, freed from their pain and suffering, and experience joy and inner healing.

There are four kinds of guests that appear in various Buddhist liturgies. First are the guests of noble refuge, the revered guests. These are the lineage gurus, tantric Buddhist deities, buddhas, and bodhisattvas. We imagine them in a huge gathering, such as Shakyamuni Buddha, Machig Labdrön and our own guru. The central deity is often specific to a liturgy. The second guests are the protectors. This mainly refers to guardian spirits—the dharmapalas who protect the sacred tradition of the Dharma, such as the four great kings. It also includes all the positive forces in the universe that protect the world, the environment, and us.

Third are the beings of the six realms. Each realm is associated with a given emotion: the hell beings are characterized by hatred; hungry ghosts, by greed; animals, by ignorance; humans, by desire; demigods, by jealousy; and the gods, or devas, by pride. These are all the beings who are not enlightened and who suffer with their own unique sorrows. They are invited to the feast with a feeling of compassion for them.

The fourth class of guests are those who are obstructers, who intentionally create obstacles to awakening. These are the beings who are in pain and malevolently and sorrowfully seek to create trouble in our lives. In the end, these are just manifestations of our minds and as such, they represent negative, self-defeating habitual patterns that jeopardize well-being and create obstacles on the spiritual path. We make sure that these guests are invited for the white and variegated feasts. Some of them are not invited to the red and black feasts.

The white feast is for accomplishing the two accumulations of wisdom and merit. It begins when our consciousness manifests as Krodha Kali and our body drops to the ground. Once the body has dropped on the ground, we point the butcher's knife toward the head of the body lying on the ground. Then the head falls off and becomes a giant skull container supported by three more skulls. Krodha Kali puts the rest of the body into the container. Then, we visualize that a fire suddenly ignites beneath the container. The fire heats the body, which then melts and turns into a porridge-like nectar. Then this nectar rains down into the sacred feast offering. The nectar blesses the offering while we chant the mantra *om āḥ hūṃ ha ho ri*. The mantra transforms the feast substance from something ordinary into a substance that can liberate the mind of anyone who tastes it. In that moment, a powerful experience happens to the practitioner energetically, which is dropping identification with the body. The complete transmutation of the body into the sacred nectar purifies all suffering and karmic patterns stored in the body consciousness. All suffering, pain, and whatever is stuck in our systems in that moment is transformed into love and liberation.

To some readers, this may sound gruesome, but it is important to appreciate it only as a ritualistic visualization whose significance is to viscerally drop the pain in the body and mind and immediately let go of ego identification with body. Even though it appears to be violent or gruesome, we can make friends with it, make peace with it, by imagining it as a sacred, benevolent surgery. Just like this, surgery uses incisive methods of cutting the body to heal us. The white feast is not meant to be gruesome but is a positive benevolent act of offering to all the buddhas and bodhisattvas with whom we have affinity. It immediately puts us in touch with our own buddha nature. By making this offering with a compassionate open heart toward all beings, the sense of separation between ourselves and other dissolves. There is a cosmic sense of relationship with all living beings. Infused with the wisdom of nonduality, guest and host are one and the two accumulations are gathered. The act of generosity brings the accumulation of merit, and nondual awareness brings the accumulation of wisdom.

In performing this feast, it is helpful to invite people and specific deities with whom we have an affinity. We invite our friends into the visualization to give them love and care, with the feeling that they need our prayers and attention. In the true spirit of altruism, we also include those with whom we have a difficult history. Through deep longing to cut all obstacles, with generosity and compassion, there can be deep healing and resolution with them.

The variegated feast visualization is the same as the beginning of the white feast. That is, consciousness shoots up out of the crowns of our heads and arises as Krodha Kali. All visualized details are the same except that once the feast has begun, clouds of steam arise from the skull cup carrying manifold offerings. Here we imagine inviting all the buddhas and bodhisattvas, as before, and every living being from everywhere without any exclusion—our friends, hungry ghosts, *nagas*, all the people we know, people we regard as our enemies, people to whom we have karmic debt, all the people in conflict with us no matter what we do, and anyone who does not like us. We invite all of them.

Arising from the nectar are the eight auspicious symbols, the symbols of universal monarchy, music, flowers, beautiful houses, jewelry, food, medicine, clothes, nice cars—all things that would be pleasing to the guests. Everybody receives just what they were looking for. They begin to enjoy themselves, and they all become satisfied. They feel that their inner hunger has finally gone, and they feel great relief. They all awaken through the power of this generosity. All the buddhas and bodhisattvas are pleased. We imagine that all our karmic debts with others are purified.

Karmic debt is the notion that we owe each other something from some point in the past. When it is not purified, it becomes an obstacle to the path and prevents us from fully living life. It holds down our consciousness from evolving. Karmic debt often shows up unexpectedly. We sometimes meet people who seem to have problems with us right from the start. They may be very irritating to us, or we may irritate them. In the beginning the connection may seem benevolent, but in the end it seems they were just creating a way to have conflict with us. We are often perplexed by this kind of situation; it is not logical. But it is a doorway. Seeing this as karmic debt can help us understand what it is all about. We can see it as a force, or energy, with someone—that we are bound together, not able to become free, with too much unfinished business. People caught in this trap can hijack each other's lives, ruffling each other's feathers constantly. The variegated feast is considered a means of purifying these karmic debts by bringing everything onto the path of healing. We imagine giving away whatever others want—medicine, clothes, shelter, a new car, the latest cell phone, whatever will completely satisfy the debtor. The visualization can be creative. It is an unconditional outpouring of whatever is needed.

The red feast is considered a means for cutting through self-grasping. The initial visualization is the same as the two previous feasts, including manifesting ourselves as Krodha Kali and visualizing that our bodies are lying on the ground as Krodha Kali points the butcher's knife toward our bodies. We visualize the body in a natural state with no adornment, no fancy clothes or jewelry, just as it is. This is a powerful means to confront, face to face, our ego or sense of separate self. The body is the very thing that we perceive as who we are. Intellectually, theoretically, we may be able to transcend our egoic identification with the body. But in everyday life, we perceive the body to be who we are. Others also relate to us as our physical appearances. It is powerful to imagine that we are suddenly this non-egoic pure awareness, as the deity Krodha Kali. This body that we have been relating to our whole lives is lying on the ground. It takes us to a powerful place of being confronted with our own ego, to deconstruct our sense of separate self, identified with the body.

As Krodha Kali we point the knife at the body beneath us and visualize the skin falling off like unfolding a rug, or a giant plate, and then as Krodha Kali we begin dissecting the body into pieces. As she does this, the whole structure of self-identification—all concepts about the body, such as pride, shame, and guilt—begins to evaporate and dissolve as ego identity is dismantled. We are left to remain as this pure awareness that cannot be defined.

Then, we bless the body as a sacred feast that has the potency to satisfy the guests and give rise to healing, freedom, and joy in the consciousness of those who taste it. We then invite the beings called *yakshas*, the meat eaters. These are mischievous spirits described in Eastern cultures as untamed, bellicose beings who travel between the human world and the spirit world. They feed on flesh and blood. We can be innovative with these images, using whatever familiar depiction we need to invoke the sense of a lower being who takes the life force from us, like a vampire. We invite beings who are hungry for flesh and thirsty for blood. They come ready to consume the feast ferociously. They represent our attachment to our egoic identity. We can also invite the enlightened beings who represent the wisdom of cutting through self-concept, such as dakinis. We imagine that they are consuming our bones and flesh and blood. Then they are all satisfied and begin to experience healing and freedom and bliss. In that moment, we allow ourselves to energetically drop the web of neurotic clinging toward self, as well as the mental construct of who we are. We become free from that chain of ego identity. The magic in this whole practice is that our body is blessed as sacred nectar and therefore has the power to liberate. That is a vital part of the feast. The yakshas are not to be taken literally as supernatural beings but are archetypal beings representing our own neuroses and ego.

The black feast is to be conducted at night. In the old days, nights were seen as a time when dark and spooky creatures came out like ghosts and zombies who push the soil away like gophers. Humans slow down and go inside at night while these formless beings roam freely. In the old days, people had a different relationship to darkness, because it was perceived as a time for the spirits. In the modern world people can hang out on the couch and read a book at night or use flashlights to run around in the dark. In cities night seems like a busy time. Nighttime can be cozy or fun. But when I was growing up in Tibet, I believed that the night was scary. We never liked the setting sun and called it the "sun of the dead."

The black feast is considered a means to purify misdeeds or negative actions causing negative karma. Negative karma is all the unwholesome things we have done, not just physically but mentally as well. They have an obstructing impact on our consciousness and become a vicious cycle, holding us back from becoming free and expansive. Whenever we act them out, the unwholesome deeds cause harm in the world around us. Once they are acknowledged, they can be purified. Though the term "negative karma" may seem judgmental, it simply describes negative actions that we may have done or negative thoughts or emotions that we have developed, that have not been purified.

Many modern people have resistance to these terms because they invoke religious ideas that seem heavy, judgmental, and dualistic. Whenever I translate Buddhist terms into English, there is always a delicate balance between not taking too much liberty and being cautious about how terms might be heard. I personally wish to avoid translating in a way that provokes negative associations. But without the concept of negative karma, we cannot have true self-awareness. So, this system is a way to put behavior and consciousness into different categories as a method to distinguish what to cultivate and what to let go of. As long as we know that the negative karma is not who we are but is simply conditions in our consciousness, which is already enlightened and perfect, then we will not fall into a holy depression or self-loathing hell because we see only the negativities.

The visualization for this feast is the same as previous visualizations, but once we become Krodha Kali we imagine that our body is lying on the ground and begins to absorb the negativities of ourselves, our loved ones, and others. Our body becomes charcoal-colored. Then we bless the body with this nectar, this divine feast that can heal and liberate anybody who tastes it. In that visualization we allow a powerful alchemical, energetic transformation. All the negativities are transmuted in pure nondual, enlightened awareness.

Then we invite the beings known as obstructers. Remember that they are merely archetypal representations of our own negativities that we have engaged with. They begin to enjoy and consume the feast and are utterly satisfied. They begin to feel bliss and that they are free from all suffering. We allow ourselves to feel the energetic release of all our negative unwholesome karma, and all negativities in our consciousness dissolve. Our whole consciousness is full of love and bliss.

Within the black feast, we also imagine that collective and ancestral karma is purified. It is important to bring about awareness of ancestral karma, which is something that is not often talked about. It is a phenomenon that needs our attention because it allows us to understand who we are and why there are certain pains and conflicts lingering in our own lives and in any given society. Many people have this awareness and try to heal and purify it. Ancestral karma can be stored in our genetic material and inherited. It comes up as pain and unresolved emotional baggage or a general family outlook that influences who we are, our state of mind, and choices we make in this life. Not only is it good for us to let go of it, but it is also good to stop transmitting these karmic patterns to the next generation. It is a blessing to us and future souls when these karmic patterns are purified and resolved.

This purification requires recognition. Through this recognition, we can understand why we experience certain states of mind, why we have pain in our lives. We can develop deep compassion for ourselves, acknowledging that we are not responsible for everything but are partially a product of ancestral karma. It will help us to understand other people as well, to see that they are just like us, also products of their ancestral karma. In this visualization, the obstructers enjoy the sacred feast and are liberated through consuming it. They are healed and release their pain. We also feel that energetic release. We feel our personal and ancestral karma has dissolved and that we are once again completely returned to the pure nature of consciousness that is already enlightened.

Often in Chöd there is a section at the end of the feast known as "giving Dharma away." We imagine that we are delivering a sacred sermon. We are teaching on love, compassion, nonviolence, and great emptiness. In this teaching, we are not speaking in the role of a guru. It is not as though we have become wise ones sitting on a high throne, but we are sharing the teachings from a mutual, equal position, offering Dharma teachings to all beings. We imagine we are encouraging the whole world to let go of hatred, love each other, and practice nonviolence. A crucial aspect of this is that we are exuding the energy of inner awakening while teaching those assembled, are also teaching the Dharma to ourselves. We are changing our state of consciousness at that moment.

In the end we imagine that all these beings are healed and satisfied and dissolve into empty space. We imagine that everything that binds us is totally dissolved into nothingness. At that time in the practice, the whole world is no longer ordinary but is a pure realm, a buddha field. It is the sacred realm of the deity Tara, and all beings are now either Avalokiteshvara or Tara. We visualize that the whole world is filled with Avalokiteshvaras and Taras, whose sacred mantras can then be chanted, helping us bring about and dwell in sacred awareness.

12

Dedication

When virtue and nonvirtue are self-liberated,
the concepts of hope and fear cannot be found.
Nonetheless, cause and effect appear as the infallible play
    of dependent arising.
I dedicate this within the pristine nature of Dharmakaya.
                                    —*The Dakini's Laughter*

Dedication is one of the most essential elements of Buddhist
practice, but some Westerners struggle with it. Many people in the East understand it easily, because it is part of the culture and they do not have to make effort to figure out what it is.
"Dedication" is a translation of the Sanskrit word *parinama*. There
are numerous liturgies and prayers pertaining to dedication, some
attributed to the Buddha and some composed by later masters.
Every Buddhist endeavor—including practices, sacred projects,
and individual practice sessions—ends with a dedication prayer.
There is a sense that without the act of dedication, some vital
aspect of practice is lacking. Dedication ensures our practice is not

tinged with ego or selfishness and is a reminder of the true purpose of such spiritual practice, which is to dedicate our spiritual practice as a cause for bringing about awakening of ourselves and all living beings, for love and compassion to grow in the hearts of all beings. Dedication permeates every aspect of Buddhist practice, especially in the Tibetan tradition.

The dedication prayer brings about a transcendent feeling that whatever we have performed has a greater value than if we were just doing it for ourselves. Dedication is a way of developing the aspiration that the merit from our practice moves the consciousness of humanity forward a bit and awakens all beings to their true nature. There are many forms of these prayers, which express the flavor of traditional practice. Spiritual practice can be dedicated to very specific causes, such as a friend's healing and healing for others who suffer the same illness. But it can also be more broadly dedicated to subjects such as world peace or prosperity for everyone. Often these prayers have slightly different flavors depending on the specific Buddhist school, expressing the central principles of each one.

Ultimately, the purpose of dedication is to make sure that we remember why we practice in the first place, which in the Mahayana is to become awakened for the benefit of everyone. For example, imagine that you are working very hard to save money to send to your brother who is very sick. You dedicate all the money earned to him. By making this dedication, you have to remember that it is for someone else, not for your own use. So, if you catch sight of a casino while driving on the highway, you remember your sick brother and do not gamble away all the money. Any spiritual practice can be tainted by ego and selfishness if there is no dedication. We are not doing spiritual practice just for ourselves. To engage with it for the purpose of personal gain would be just another way to perpetuate selfishness. Without dedication, we can also begin to reify the results of practice. Mahayana Buddhism, which is the basis of Chöd, has a view to bring about enlightenment not only for ourselves but for others and for the world.

Dedication of merit prevents attachment to practice because whatever is gained from it is offered, and it becomes something that has been done with an unselfish motivation. Our tradition is that when someone dies, monks are invited to chant prayers and people offer hundreds of butter lamps for the deceased one. These lamps are offered to the buddhas and bodhisattvas, and their flames represent illuminating wisdom. When anyone offers a butter lamp, they are supposed to keep in mind that it represents inner wisdom and make an aspiration prayer with that understanding, saying, for example, "May all beings be illuminated by the light of wisdom." The dedication that follows is an act of bringing this aspiration to fruition.

Many lay people may not know how to hold an unconditioned aspiration for the welfare of beings. There is a wild, true story of a nomadic family in Tibet that lost one of the parents and invited monks to do a butter lamp ceremony. One of the monks performing the ceremony overheard one of the nomads saying, "I dedicate this butter lamp only to my mother, not to anybody else." This is an example of reifying the dedication, because he was turning the merit into a commodity. He thought he could pick and choose who received the benefits of his offering, rather than letting go of grasping and clinging to the outcome. By believing that the virtue of practice would be lessened if it were shared with many people, he misunderstood the heart of dedication. You are not just holding the virtue for yourself but are sharing the benefit and blessing of your spiritual practice with endless others, with all sentient beings. This is why we dedicate everything for a higher universal purpose.

All Vajrayana practices end with a dedication prayer. Whatever benefit has arisen through the two accumulations during practice increases through the process of dedicating. The dedication in Chöd is done in order to go beyond the chain of the eight worldly concerns so that all beings are free from the grips of the four maras. The maras are anything that hinders us from awakening to our true nature. These may include our mental projections and emotional baggage—anything that creates obstacles to spiritual practice and inner development. Through dedication, we aspire to be free from the prison of self-grasping, from anything that prevents us from becoming awakened or causes us to be taken over by the maras that chain our heart and mind to the finite.

Dedicating the fruition of our practice can ultimately lead to realizing great emptiness. In the end, since it is all about letting go of attachment to everything including the practice itself, in the same vein, we have to let go of even the dedication itself. This is the highest version of true nondual dedication in which we transcend the notions "I am the dedicator," "Someone is going to receive this dedication," and "There is an act of dedicating." This is the highest form of dedication, free from clinging to the concepts of subject, object, and action. There is no act of dedicating, no object of dedication, and no dedicator. This is the heart of nondual, nonconceptual dedication that is inexhaustible and unfettered by self-grasping.

Dedication is a form of generosity, even though you are not giving material objects but rather the merit and virtue from the Dharma. You are giving away the merit to everybody and it has an immediate impact on your consciousness of expanding the heart into pure joy, charity, love, and kindness. You are released from the habitual energetic grasping of ego, and this causes the expression of joy in generosity.

In Chöd we dedicate the Dharma to all living beings. Maintaining a loving connection with everyone, the merit can expand to the whole world. Such generosity comes with a feeling of love and compassion toward others and becomes one of those moments when we can really love everyone without partiality. Meditation practice generates a very positive feeling, and at the conclusion, this is given away. Through this, something very beautiful and exquisite is shared with the whole world, and consequently a positive and rich connection to the world is ripened. The state of the world often makes it difficult to do this. This completely vast aspiration creates a connection between us and the world as a source of awakening and love. Any action undertaken, any positive thought that occurs, any beneficial event—all of these can be dedicated to the welfare of others.

Dedication does not just have to do with the context of sadhana practice. You can dedicate anything that you think of as positive, anything done in goodness or regarded as meritorious. That merit can be dedicated. For example, giving a penny to a homeless person, when done with the spirit of generosity, expresses intrinsic basic goodness. In his first inaugural address, Abraham Lincoln borrowed Shakespeare's phrase, saying, "The mystic chords of memory, stretching from every battlefield and patriot grave to every living heart and hearthstone all over this broad land, will yet swell the chorus of the Union, when again touched, as surely they will be, by the better angels of our nature."

There is goodness in each of us, which he calls the "better angel." This inherent, noble goodness aims to not always serve ourselves but to serve a greater purpose. It empowers us to do things for the sake of others. Seeing a homeless person, some inner angel motivates us to donate. We can see this human being as our brother or sister and give to them. In Buddhism, this is the virtue of *kusala*. Kusala is the skillfulness of not doing things that prevent spiritual development and focusing efforts on actions that bring it about. Dedication is natural. It is about the human principle, the better angels in each of us.

Dedication may sound transcendent and abstract, but it is not. It is based on the ground of love and compassion, with being engaged with the world. It comes along with awareness of the very specific needs of the world: political, social, and health-related needs, along with all forms of suffering in the world. A very famous example of the dedication prayer is the tenth chapter of Shantideva's *The Way of the Bodhisattva*. By reciting the chapter, we immediately experience the spirit and breadth of aspiration within the act of dedication. Each verse dedicates the virtue of the bodhisattva for benefiting all beings, such as to end suffering in all worlds, conceivable and inconceivable. The bodhisattva's aspiration is for the enlightenment of all, to free them from suffering. Bodhisattvas must dedicate all of their virtue so that all beings will be freed from their vices and live in virtue and ease.

The practice of dedication is not abstract but often accomplished with discernment and awareness of what is happening in the world. Shantideva was a man of his time and a true bodhisattva. He was aware of the hardships of the times. When he makes the wish "that this woman will be able to give birth with ease," it is from a place of understanding the hazards and joys of childbirth. Celebration of a new baby could easily turn to sorrow and struggle, since there were no modern interventions or medicine. In those times, primitive conditions often led to the death of infants and mothers due to complications that are easily addressed now. If someone heard you chanting a dedication for a woman's easy delivery in today's world, they may think it strange. But back then birth was full of many difficulties, and Shantideva's dedication for women to give birth easily was meaningful. This is in alignment with the bodhisattva who does everything to help others with completely impartial love. Shantideva then dedicates his bodhisattva practice to make sure hungry ones get food and poor ones get material possessions. He makes a prayer that everyone will enjoy prosperity in the world.

Dedication shows that the bodhisattva is not just lost in a false transcendence of ideas but demonstrates the breadth and unconditioned quality of aspiration. By establishing the fullest possible field of aspiration for bodhisattva practice, Shantideva shows the boundless nature of his own compassion and his wish to have everyone practice this way. Dedication is not an abstract thing but is full of awareness and consciousness of sociopolitical issues. In one verse, he dedicates the virtue of the bodhisattva for the nuns to find sustenance. In most ancient cultures, women were less respected than men and nuns were less respected than monks. Monks did not work for a living but dedicated their whole lives to contemplation and spiritual practices, receiving sustenance, donations, and great reverence from the lay community. Now and then the state had policies supporting their sustenance. By contrast, many lay people believed monks were holier than nuns, donated less to them, and left them struggling for basic necessities. They thought donating to the monks would create more blessings than offering to the nuns. This is not a Buddhist idea but just human ignorance. Buddhism does not determine a hierarchy; it is pure in itself and transcends a limited understanding about the nature of all things. But when practiced, Buddhism is often mixed with our own ignorance or confusion. What results is far from Buddhist teachings. This is why monks were believed to generate more merit and blessings and so received more donations. Because Shantideva was aware of this, he included the nuns in this chapter, making the dedication that nuns would have sustenance. He says, "May nuns have all their wants supplied."

Dedication is not just a mechanical practice but rouses our aspiration, love, compassion, and caring for the world. When I practice with groups, I invite everyone to dedicate the goodness that comes from it to others' awakening and to make specific dedications to current issues, such as ending violence and injustice, while sending wishes for healing, harmony, peace, and prosperity to everyone everywhere. Just like Shantideva, dedication is a moment when we can bring about awareness to pressing sociopolitical issues that need attention. Sometimes, spirituality is detached from issues like climate change and inequality to avoid the discomfort of these struggles and discord, but at some point they have to be included, because this is how we can give rise to true compassion and love. We are not just cultivating some beautiful, intellectual ideal. This powerful method brings everyone's attention to important issues that need to be addressed and should not be ignored. From this, awareness of the issues is implanted in everybody's minds, so ultimately our cumulative efforts bring about change for the better.

Inequality, like the nuns of old experienced, has not gone away. Many experience it as having become a bigger issue around the world, in rich and poor countries. Inequality takes dignity away from people who are less fortunate and creates an invisible caste system. Consecrated by the gods of capitalism and materialism, it also keeps the powerful and wealthy from knowing how to feel content. Powerful institutions like police forces and governments indirectly create and maintain the modern caste system. I do not think the world is going to be a good place for humanity until this issue is tackled. A shocking statistic states that a very small percent of our population owns most of the wealth of the world: sixty families own one half the world's wealth! There is a kind of insanity in the world when there is such extreme inequality. A simple example is of a billionaire whose dining room doors are made of solid gold while millions around the world cannot eat. Inequality is a problem because many people have lived in privilege and have no awareness of it. As we become more aware, our hearts can open and we can dedicate our practice to the impoverished and disenfranchised in order to end the disparity and suffering.

Though many multibillionaires share a philanthropic ethic, there is an argument that some of them are sharing their merit simply to receive the crown of "philanthropist" or perhaps just to feel good. Though there are a few examples of individuals with genuine care for the world, most contribute only a tiny percent of their total wealth for the benefit of others. The businesses that made them wealthy cause damage to the environment and take advantage of workers. The way they run their empires may contribute to social inequality. Though they may have aspirations to change the world, they are often blind to the nature of inequality itself.

We want to see a world where everyone is respected, where everyone has their dignity. We are not talking about an idealistic utopia where everyone has the same bank account but rather dedicating our heart and mind to eradicate this extreme, pathological inequality. During the dedication, we offer all virtues and benefit of practice to everyone in the world, wishing that they have equality and dignity. Then our whole practice is authentic and helps expand consciousness further and further.

In Tibet Chöd practice is done for emotional and physical healing. In early 2020, the COVID-19 pandemic was spreading all over the world, quickly hitting the United States. There were widespread political demonstrations and erupting anger regarding social justice and racial issues. In this context, it felt like a good time to do Chöd practice to overcome the illness and heal social trauma. It felt that Chöd was the right medicine. Therefore, my friends and I felt the need to do something in addition to our other social and political activities, so we started doing more *Dakini's Laughter* Chöd practice. We often got together with friends in virtual practice sessions. In my mind, I dedicated the practice to bring about healing and end the pandemic.

Initially, I was resistant to virtual practice because I had never done it before. It felt artificial. Shortly after, however, I realized

that it was the only choice for how to come together. As we settled into the routine of these practice sessions, we began to feel
the magic of our connection. Though technology stood between
us, I felt that we dropped into completely inspired and intimate
connection to each other, feeling that the power of shared practice
overcame the limits of this medium and of our physical distance.
Every time I engage in the dedication section of the practice, I feel
we are doing it to bring about healing and reconciliation, embracing our global aspiration to sooth the trauma in our world. Our
community feels this is the right thing to do.

APPENDIX: MACHIG'S RADICAL PATH

There is no need to offer a lengthy introduction to Machig Labdrön, since she is not an obscure character in the history of Tibetan Buddhism. She is one of the most well-known Tibetan Buddhist masters, and there are several scholarly books written about her life. But as she is central to Chöd practice, I would like to illustrate some pivotal periods in her life that defined her and inspired her to develop the practice of Chöd.

Machig Labdrön was unique in Tibetan history. She was one of few recognized female Vajrayana masters active in Tibet after Yeshe Tsogyal (the first female Buddhist master from the eighth century) and also founded a unique version of the radical path of Chöd. Her new tradition has been inspiring devoted practitioners for centuries.

Chöd is a powerful reflection of her path as a woman who developed a deep understanding of the Prajnaparamita sutras and who was also a devout Vajrayana practitioner. Over the centuries, Buddhism spread through spoken teachings, scriptures, and vision transmissions, making its way to the raw landscape of Tibet. Machig Labdrön transcended all sectarian boundaries and is recognized as a mahasiddha by everyone in the Tibetan Buddhist world. Her full name was Machig Labgyi Drönma. Machig means "the only, sole mother." "Lab" identifies that she is from the Lab region of western Tibet. Within the name Drönma, "Drön" means lamp. Many female masters and nuns are given the name Drönma, and it is also found in many scriptures. It is an analogy of the power of Dharma that dispels inner darkness. This was not her birth name or her only name, though. One of her other names was given to her by the family chaplain, Jowo Dampa, who tutored her in reading complex texts. When by eight years old she had mastered these, Jowo Dampa recognized that her wisdom was as brilliant as a fire spreading in a great forest. So he suggested that her parents call her Sherab Drönme, meaning "lamp of wisdom."

Monastics and the privileged were typically the only twelfth-century Tibetans to become literate. Because of her noble family, she was fortunate to be taught to read by her mother and a tutor and began reading by age five. During those times, there was no separation between Buddhist and secular education. When people learned how to read, the Buddhist texts and scriptures were their reading material. With her uncommon brilliance, Machig Labdrön's early accomplishment in reading must have encouraged her parents to continue her education. This was already unusual, as few women in her time learned how to read. It was most common for those who learned to read to become monks and lamas.

By age eight, under Jowo Dampa's tutelage, Machig Labdrön could read and write and was practiced in recitation. By ten years old, she began showing particular skill in voice modulation for fast reading. In Tibet, it is traditional for villages, towns, and monasteries to host monastics to read long Buddhist sacred texts as ceremonies for purposes such as funerals and healings. There were some monks and nuns who could read very fast. It is said that some could read as much as six times faster than the average person. These fast readers were rare, but Machig Labdrön was one of them.

At an early age, Machig Labdrön began to be revered in the community as a sort of sublime being. People began asking for her blessings and offering her prostrations, suspecting that she was an emanation of a great bodhisattva. Mahayana Buddhism's foundation of benefiting all beings holds that great buddhas and bodhisattvas will choose to reincarnate in this human world to help others. When someone such as Machig Labdrön has deep kindness and understanding of the Mahayana teachings, it is common for lay people to believe that this person is a reincarnate bodhisattva. Her reputation as a fast reader and an exceptional being were widespread.

While she was still quite young, a powerful local king threw a huge celebration, welcoming everyone. The king had heard of her reputation, and he invited several well-known scholars and monks. Doubting that she was as accomplished as her reputation indicated, the king asked her to read for everyone to show her exceptional skill. As she read, her brilliance and skill were immediately evident, so he no longer doubted her. The king's approval then caused others' respect and appreciation for her to grow.

When Machig Labdrön turned thirteen, her mother passed away. This reinforced her desire to pursue a spiritual path. She went to study with a teacher named Geshe Atön and for three years received complete instruction in the tenets and scriptures of the Mahayana, including the Prajnaparamita, the transcendent wisdom. Machig Labdrön immersed herself in her studies and surpassed her teacher's and his disciples' understanding. Geshe Atön was sincere in supporting her development, so he sent her to someone who could nurture her growth and understanding. At age sixteen, she went to study with a teacher named Drapa Ngönshechen, or Lama Drapa, who had profound understanding of many doctrines and practices. He very quickly recognized her exceptional ability to recite sutras and invited her to be his chaplain and recite scriptures for his community. Under the guidance and instruction of Lama Drapa, she developed great realization of the profound meaning of the Mahayana Buddhist writings that describe the path of bodhisattvas and their realization of *mahashunyata,* the great emptiness.

It is important for us to remember that Machig Labdrön was more than just another enlightened master. She was exceptional because it was so uncommon for a woman to gain this level of reverence from scholars and to have the chance to study and develop such penetrating spiritual insight into the scriptures. This was partly because society did not allow women to actualize their full potential, as they were mostly relegated to childbearing and homemaking. The depth of her understanding and her fearless commitment to practice stand as testimony to how unique she was.

Given Buddhism's origins, Tibetans tend to regard Indian masters as the sources of reliable understanding on finer points of philosophy and scripture. During those days, Tibetans often sought Indian masters to clarify their questions or doubts about Buddhist doctrine. These Indian teachers were in high demand. One such Indian master revered by Tibetans was Padampa Sangye, or Dampa Sangye, a great siddha who visited Tibet many times during his extensive travels. He also had insight into the traps of scholasticism, recognizing that if consciousness is stuck in mere conceptual understanding, it could remain unaffected by the knowledge it held. Padampa often encouraged disciples not to mistake intellect with wisdom or scholasticism with true awakening. He was a humble free spirit, having cut through attachment to mundane glory. He was not born with a silver spoon in his mouth and did not have a huge estate or attendants. Instead, he walked his talk, forsaking material displays of his inner awakening.

Padampa Sangye journeyed extensively through Tibet, India, China, and Nepal. Because he traveled unadorned with a carefree simple demeanor and lived without fame, power, or prestige, people often dismissed him and did not recognize him as a spiritual teacher. One time a famous Tibetan translator was staying at the same guesthouse in Nepal as Padamapa. The translator thought he was a servant and asked him, "Who is your master?" Padampa, instead of being insulted, wittily replied, "I'm a servant to all beings."

On another trip en route from India to Tibet, Padampa joined two Tibetan pilgrims who were returning home from Nepal. One of the Tibetans was a monk who had gone to India and Nepal seeking Buddhist teachings but also to learn to perform magic. He was holding an ornately carved wooden stick decorated with animal totems for the purpose of performing magic. The Tibetans had no idea who Padampa was or that he was a great teacher. However, an Indian merchant they encountered immediately recognized Padampa Sangye and began bowing, offering him prostrations. The Tibetans took notice of this and opened their eyes to look more deeply at their traveling companion, finally seeing that he was an extraordinary spiritual master. At some point he approached the lama with the stick and said, "Your ornate stick is just a tool for magic but will not be of benefit in true awakening. Were you planning to use it to deceive Tibetans?" He then grabbed the stick and broke it on his knee, showing that he did not rely on spiritual trickery aimed only at gaining donations. His interest was solely teaching the true Dharma.

The age of twenty was a milestone in Machig Labdrön's spiritual path. During this year, she completed her four-year commitment as a reader for Lama Drapa's monastery and also met two teachers, Padampa Sangye and Kyotön Sönam Dragpa, who would influence the depth and direction of the rest of her life. As discussed in chapter 2, Padampa Sangye recognized that she was an advanced being and gave her his seven axioms.

After her first meeting with Padampa Sangye, she met Sönam Dragpa, also known as Sönam Lama. He was adept in many philosophical systems and a guru to many monks. Yet he had decided to turn inward, let go of his position, and become a wandering yogi. He renounced his fame, fortune, and position in the truest sense. Perhaps moved by his example, his complete renunciation, and his devotion to yogic discipline, Machig Labdrön eventually abandoned her position and fame. She must have recognized in him that mere accomplishment in scholastics, monastic discipline, and intellectual understanding were not the main goal of the journey. Though she was a great scholar, she must have felt the limits of her accomplishments, inspiring her to go beyond the confines of her familiar milieu.

Sönam Dragpa challenged her to deepen her understanding and realization, saying, "You are so adept at the words of Prajnaparamita, but do you understand their meaning? Please explain the meaning of the sutras." Machig Labdrön gave a thorough elucidation of the Prajnaparamita sutras, to which he answered, "You understand their meaning, but it seems the meaning has not yet ripened in your mindstream." With this pointing out, she humbly asked how she might ripen the teachings within herself. He replied, "Everything you just spoke is called 'intellectual understanding,' yet the meaning of these teachings has not been realized. The moment your understanding of these teachings ripens in your mindstream, then a new insight will occur in you. At that moment, you will lose all reference points and be free from concepts. The great fire of wisdom of non-doing will blaze, destroying the darkness of unawareness and self-grasping."

From that moment on, she began to internalize her understanding, such that her mind became free from the chain of conceptual fixation. On reading the section on maras in the Prajnaparamita sutras, she experienced a profound awakening, after which all reference points and self-grasping dissolved.

During this period of time, she felt that she needed to go through a radical change in her life, truly let go of her attachment to worldly affairs, and continuously allow her inner awakening to grow. Before that, she wore fancy clothes, but afterward she wore the clothes of a beggar, which is a sign that she had transcended attachment to appearance. Before that, she only related to adept practitioners, such as abbots, masters, monks, and nuns. Afterward, she sought company with lepers and beggars. This is a sign of transcending attachment to friends. Before that, she only stayed in her monastery and hermitage, but afterward she would stay anywhere, in the home of lepers or on the road. This is sign of transcending attachment to place or residence. Before that, she only lived in limited regions—comfort zones. Afterward she went everywhere. This was a sign that partiality and direction were transcended. Before that, she only ate a vegetarian diet, known as "three whites and three sweets," but from there on she would eat any food, good or bad, even if it came from the hands of lepers. This shows that she transcended her attachment to food. Before that, she preferred praise, respect, and comfort. But from then on, she became fearless in the face of insult, blame, and criticism from her enemies and friends. Sorrow and joy became the same. She did not have any unhappiness from that time on.

Her reputation and fame as an awakened yogini and an insightful, knowledgeable scholar continued to grow. For example, she was invited to debate seven well-known scholar-monastics. The subject they were to debate was the Prajnaparamita. The art of debate continues to be a big part of the Tibetan Buddhist monastic tradition, just as it had been in India. Machig Labdrön excelled in using it to sharpen her understanding of the Dharma. Each opponent in debate conceded to her superior understanding of the subtleties of Dharma, catapulting her to a sort of holy stardom. She remained a celibate ascetic for quite a long time, due to her total dedication to the spiritual path, in which worldly affairs were not of interest to her. But as she developed spiritually, her inner awakening led her to return to worldly affairs and embrace human life fully, integrating her Dharma path with ordinary life.

She met a wandering Indian yogi named Töpa Bhadra, who is described in biographies as being unique looking with bloodshot eyes. In those days, most Tibetans had never met someone from another culture or race, so they took notice of his looks. He was also a scholar, and they got to know each other through conversations on Buddhist doctrine. They soon fell in love and consummated their relationship. Given her pure lifestyle and spiritual pursuit, she was challenged by the romance, so she consulted her teachers Drapa Ngönshechen and Kyotön Sönam Drakpa. Both assured her that she should pursue her new path, offering their blessings for her to have a family and children. At the age of twenty-four, she gave birth to her first child. She and Töpa Bhadra raised four children.

When they first married, there was controversary because her contemporaries felt she had fallen from grace by giving up her life as a renunciant. They moved to a new region perhaps as a way to escape from the harsh gossip. But her two teachers loyally supported her through every turn, continually giving their blessings, and showing their support for her decisions. Their recognition of her supreme integrity and deep commitment to her path is fully expressed in their blessings. Most importantly, they regarded her as a mahasiddha, a yogini who had attained the highest levels of attainment.

Though most Buddhist practices are from India, her form of Chöd was unique in being a Tibetan practice. Machig Labdrön herself said, "All Dharmas in Tibet come from India. My Dharma is the only one that went from Tibet back to India." Because Buddhism had flourished in India for centuries before being planted in the Land of Snow, Indians often looked upon Tibetans as young students. To this day, when there is a doctrinal conflict between Tibetan scholars, these conflicts are resolved by consulting original Indian scriptures for essential and correct interpretation. Machig Labdrön's biography tells us that in her time there were Indian panditas who heard news of a woman teacher in Tibet called Machig Labdrön who taught a Dharma called Chöd. They felt they had to check and make sure she was teaching the true Dharma, so they sent Indian scholars all the way to Tibet to debate with her. In the end, the Indian Buddhists accepted her Chöd teachings as true Dharma. The Indian Buddhists were inspired by Chöd, which was a sign that Tibetan Buddhism had become fully mature and independent and no longer needed to rely on Indian reference points. This is a vital milestone in the history of Buddhism.

Today Machig Labdrön's writings stand as a living testimony to her brilliance and enlightenment. They reveal the depth and profundity of her wisdom and amply underscore why establishing Chöd as a tradition and lineage made her one of the most revered and important masters in Tibetan Buddhism. Machig Labdrön's profound contribution is incorporated into every major Tibetan Buddhist sect. Chöd has flourished since its inception, like the continuing spread of Buddhism since the time of Shakyamuni Buddha.

Dharmata
FOUNDATION

Dharmata Foundation carries the current inventory of Anam Thubten's books and recorded teachings through their online bookstore.

Anam Thubten travels widely to teach and conduct meditation retreats in many locations across the US and abroad. For more information, a schedule of Dharmata events, and access to the bookstore, please visit:

www.dharmata.org
Other inquiries may be directed to:
info@dharmata.org

Dharmata Foundation
235 Washington Avenue
Point Richmond, California 94801

ABOUT THE AUTHOR

Anam Thubten grew up in Tibet and at an early age began to practice in the Nyingma tradition of Tibetan Buddhism. He is the founder and spiritual advisor of the Dharmata Foundation, and he teaches widely in the United States and internationally. He is the author of *Choosing Compassion*; *No Self, No Problem*; *The Magic of Awareness*; and *Embracing Each Moment*.

To view Anam Thubten's teaching and retreat schedule, please visit www.dharmata.org.